The Catholic Faith:
An Introduction

The Catholic Faith:
An Introduction

Lawrence S. Cunningham

PAULIST PRESS
New York/Mahwah

Library of Congress Cataloging-in-Publication Data

Cunningham, Lawrence.
    The Catholic faith.

    Bibliography: p.
    1. Catholic Church—Doctrines.   I. Title.
BX1751.2.C86   1987   282   86-25450
ISBN 0-8091-2859-4 (pbk.)

Published by Paulist Press
997 Macarthur Boulevard
Mahwah, New Jersey 07430

Printed and bound in the
United States of America

Contents

Introduction

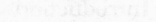

Some years ago I complained to an editor of Paulist Press that there was no decent single volume introduction to Catholicism that one could put into the hands of young college students. Being an editor, he challenged me to write one. The challenge remained in the back of my mind but other duties and other obligations set up roadblocks in my way. Since I first uttered that complaint a number of such introductions have appeared ranging from the comprehensive to the barest of outlines. Why add to the list? The lofty answer is that the subject of Catholicism is so vast and so inexhaustible that one could always add to the books about it without fear of repetition. The more mundane reason is that over the years I have approached the subject of Catholicism in my own way and had accumulated a fair pile of notes and jottings which, with some little effort, could be turned into a book. So when, with the aid of a sabbatical, I had the time and leisure, I sat down to sketch out a book using my own notes and my own experiences in the classroom.

I say that it is "my" book. That is only partially true. As the notes and bibliography attest, my indebtedness to any number of writers is manifest. The influence of Karl Rahner is patent both because he was the premier theologian of our age and because I immensely admire the originality of his thought as it was wedded to a profoundly deep love for the Church and its tradition. The book also owes much to those quizzical looks, agnostic arches of the eyebrow, and sighs of disagreement that have come from my students over the years. One can bully their disagreements into silence in class but their critiques demand that one refine and restate for greater clarity and a fairer presentation of things. It is also nice to have congenial colleagues with just enough competitiveness in them to keep one working if only to maintain one's self-respect. It is even nicer to have a departmental chairman like Walter L. Moore, Jr. who finds one breathing space to work and nurtures one's labors with kindness and professionalism.

Robert Heyer (now of Leaven Press) first encouraged this book. I got much kind support from Father Kevin Lynch while it was being written. Douglas Fisher nurtured the book into print. Dianne Weinstein typed the manuscript with her usual skill and good will. I would like to thank all of them for their kindnesses.

Cecilia Davis Cunningham is friend, wife, mother, and artist extraordinary. This book is for her.

Chapter I

Approaching Catholicism: A First Word

Catholicism must seem an exasperating and bewildering phenomenon if it is only known from a reading of the newspapers or from viewing television. How does one get any sense of the whole when bombarded by pictures of religious processions in Poland, rosary sayers before abortion clinics in Cleveland, advertisements for bingo held at the local parish hall, figures like Mother Teresa in India and the Pope in Rome, priests who write racy novels, nuns who protest submarine launchings, St. Patrick's Day parades, bloody quarrels in Ulster, Marxist Catholics in Central America, religious sisters or priests espousing God knows what on Phil Donahue? Those are only a handful of conspicuous happenings which may make it into the media. Within the Catholic family one must account for parochial schools, religious statues, the Vatican, the local bishop, birth control, clergy who cannot marry (but sometimes do), and so on.

This religious complexity has often bemused those who were born and raised in the Church. As a kid growing up in the deep south I rather envied the simple church style of my overwhelmingly Baptist neighbors. They had a church, a preacher, a Bible, a few doctrines, two ordinances, and a straightforward service: sing, pray, listen to the Bible readings and the preacher's sermon, and go home. We, by contrast, had this bewildering array of clergy (bishops, two kinds of monsignors, pastors, curates, monks, nuns, etc.), churches (cathedrals, shrines, parishes, missions, etc.), a complex set of beliefs (they had heaven and hell; we added limbo and purgatory), seven sacraments, and a very complex worship service that was all in Latin to boot.

So our first question is this: Is there something beneath (or behind) this complex phenomenon called Catholicism that holds it all together and gives it a certain logic? Is there something like a set of Catholic first principles from which everything else flows or, at least, which helps to make sense of everything else?

The answer is "yes" and it is one of the purposes of this book to elaborate on that "yes." We hope, in short, to provide an entry into that complex reality called Catholicism.* Our intention is to keep a

---

*We use the term "Catholicism" to mean Roman Catholic and not as a theological category

steady eye on those basics which form the foundation of Catholicism and against which everything else is either explained or judged.

We wish to stay with the basics for a very good and simple reason. An anecdote might help to explain why. As a professor of religion with a special interest in things Catholic I am often asked—sometimes with an edge of challenge but more often with an air of puzzlement—how Catholics can be against birth control or "for" purgatory or hostile to a married clergy or . . . (fill in the blank). When questioned in that fashion I often sigh with resigned bemusement, since I know that none of those issues can make any sense at all unless they are understood against a very large backdrop of historical development and doctrinal evolution. Birth control—to pick the most vexatious issue—is unintelligible without an understanding of the Catholic understanding of anthropology, marriage, social ethics, etc. One cannot even see that it is a serious issue worthy of discussion unless one can enter into the larger worldview of the Church.

It is only after an understanding, then, of what Catholicism stands for as a basic religious worldview that "Catholic" issues make any sense. For that reason we want to start with those bedrock principles and beliefs.

To further specify what we are about here let me make two other preliminary observations which are (a) what this book does *not* intend to do and (b) what it does hope to do.

This work is not designed as an encyclopedia of Catholic trivia. If one desires to know the difference between the brown and green scapular (or even what a scapular is), the origin of fast days, the various species of prelates, and so on, this is not the book to read. Nor will this book attempt a comprehensive overview of all Catholic belief and practice. It would be otiose to redo Richard McBrien's *Catholicism*** which, in two volumes, gives us a synoptic but generous coverage of those matters. Finally, this book will try to stay very close to the observable reality of the Church as it is. We have very fine books available about the way the Church should be or might be in a better world or as derived from a better set of theological principles. I do not intend to indulge in such visionary schemas.

which has a wider and more ecumenical sense. It will almost always be a descriptive term in this book unless otherwise noted.

**Footnotes in the book will be kept to a decent minimum. A select and annotated bibliography is at the end of the volume.

What we will attempt is to provide an account, as fully as space allows, of the texture of the Catholic experience and the bases for that experience. I imagine an audience that will consist of interested non-Roman Catholics as well as Catholics who might inquire into questions such as: What is Catholicism all about? And, following on that question, why Catholicism and not something else?

In attempting to answer those questions we will make constant reference to those things which the sympathetic questioner might easily experience: the daily life of the parish, the stories of the Bible, and what common culture tells us of Catholicism. We will try not to be heavily "theological" in the sense that it will not be a treatment of Catholicism which is overly speculative. We will make generous use of what theologians write and cite their work where apposite. To use Andrew Greeley's phrase, we will be consumers, rather than producers, of theology.

The suspicious reader might well inquire about the author's intellectual point of departure. Will this book be a "conservative" one or will it be "liberal" or what? What are the author's biases? The latter should reveal themselves in the course of the work but the former question might better be answered in a somewhat parenthetical manner. Every Sunday (Saturday evening, actually) I trudge over to the local parish for Mass as I have done for most of my life. On workdays I usually can be found in my office at the university. The rest of the time I spend within the comfortable confines of family life. Life in a family and in a parish nourishes me with a sense of continuity and tradition. It makes me want to conserve. Life in the university—where, as Newman says, the clash of mind with mind should take place—tends to make me intellectually suspicious. The upshot of all this—the one autobiographical flicker I shall ignite in this book—is that the author will treat this subject with prickly love and a kind of cranky fidelity which is sometimes identified with faith.

The Character of Catholicism

As an introduction to the whole I should like to begin with five general observations and say a few words about each:

(1) Catholicism is a religious tradition;

(2) that tradition is Christian;

(3) that Christian tradition expresses itself as a community;

(4) that community expresses a worldview;

(5) that worldview is best described as a "Catholic" one.

I understand religion here in that generic sense once assigned it by the Roman writer, Cicero: religion (from the Latin *religare*—to bind) is that which binds us to the divine. By further describing religion as a tradition we further specify that this "binding to God" has a history behind it. Tradition means a "handing down" and, by implication, the act of remembering. So, when we say that Catholicism is a religious tradition, we are saying, in essence, that it is a way of relating to God which has a history to it, a history which has generations behind it as well as a collective memory.

This religious tradition is Christian. The Christian character of Catholicism can be understood in a number of senses. In its broadest sense, Christian simply means that in the spectrum of world religions Catholicism is not a part of Hinduism or Buddhism or Islam or Judaism. More specifically it means that Christianity looks back to that person named Jesus who lived in a specific moment of history. Catholics, like most Christians, claim that that man named Jesus who was called the Christ (the term Christ, from the Greek word for "one who is anointed," translates the Hebrew term *messiah*) was the unique revelation of God in history, and that same Jesus, named the Christ, is the Savior of the world. Those claims are so sweeping, so audacious, and so paradoxically startling that it could be said that to fully explore those claims alone would reveal the very heart of Christianity in general and Catholicism in particular.

At the very heart of Christianity, then, is not a teaching, but a person—a person who makes unique and startling claims. It is likewise true that were one to remove that person the very heart of Catholicism would be dead. But we must hasten to add that Catholicism understands that person in a peculiar and unique fashion. Baptists, Methodists, Greek Orthodox, Anglicans, and a host of other religious bodies within Christianity would state—and rightly so—that Jesus the Christ is at the center of their religious belief and practice. Our task, then, would seem to be a dual one: to set out an understanding of Jesus the Christ as he is commonly understood by Christianity in general (if, indeed, one could make such generalizations) and then to outline the understanding of Christ in the context of the Catholic tradition. That latter is crucial since, as we shall see, the traditional understanding of Christ, to a very crucial degree, shapes the Catholic understanding of human nature, the Church, the sacraments, and the Catholic approach to the general destiny of human culture. For that reason one of our most basic questions must be that same one first raised by Jesus himself in the Gospels: "What think ye of the Christ?"

We have also said that this Christian religious tradition is also a community. By community we mean both a union with God in Christ and a union with others of like faith and persuasion. We can think of this community for now as a bond between people who share a common set of beliefs and practices and who symbolize that bond by shared ritual activity. One could read reams of pages on Catholicism and learn less about community than by a simple and sympathetic observance of the social and religious functions of a typical Catholic parish. While there is a wide scope of spiritual opportunities in the Church as a whole, it is most often in the local community (which, at least in North America, means the parish) where the parameters of Catholic life are best observed.

The Catholic sense of community manifests itself in quite different ways and with varying levels of intensity and commitment. The average Catholic finds that primary sense of community in his or her worshiping community, but to be a Catholic means to be a member both of the local community and somehow part of that "Great Church" whose visible center is in Rome. When one has divided the community into local and universal (i.e., my parish and the Roman see), there are still all kinds of community bonds which may bind us together at different levels in between. Belonging to a monastic or religious order is a form of community; participating in a prayer group or a Bible study circle within or outside the parish is another; membership in a voluntary association like the Legion of Mary or the St. Vincent De Paul Society may yet be a third. In other words, within that large community which we may call the Church of Rome there are any number of smaller communities which provide a sense of intimacy and sharing. What brings all of these smaller communities into one is a shared sense of communion, understanding and linkage with the Great Church. The Catholic sense of community at once resists a parochialism which sees only the local community as normative or which emphasizes a kind of amorphous universalism. Catholic community honors the household of the faith in both its local and its universal manifestation.

The Catholic sense of community honors both the present community of believers and the past members who now, in the words of the liturgy "sleep the sleep of peace." By keeping alive its memory of the saints, by reciting its ancient creeds, by participation in a liturgy whose structure is ancient, by praying for its dead—in all of these gestures we affirm a community which is not only actual but rooted in the memory of history. By cherishing its collective memory Catholics stand in solidarity with its past and its associations with that past.

We say further that this Catholic community has a "worldview." By that term we simply mean that Catholicism looks at the "big issues" from a definite point of view. The general contours of that worldview are easy enough to state. It does not regard the universe as cold, randomly organized, or an indifferent place. It sees meaning and structure in the world. It regards people as neither angels nor beasts. It sees humanity as noble and created by God but, at the same time, as flawed and in need of healing. Indeed, it sees the deep human longing for wholeness and completeness as the deep source of its own meaning. To be human, Catholicism would insist, is, in the last analysis, to be religious.

In its worldview Catholicism takes history very seriously. Indeed, as we shall see in some detail, it is fundamental to Catholic self-understanding that the history of the people of Israel be seen as a sacred history and that Jesus be considered as someone who entered human history. Because of its insistence on the importance of history and the historical process, Catholicism is (or ideally should be) committed to being in this world which it sees as the proper arena of religious activity. The great paradox of Catholicism is that it is in, but not of, the world. Its insertion in history impels Catholicism to be a religion of realism— sensitive to human needs, human aspirations, and human destiny. That is why the Catholic Church could affirm, in the words of the Second Vatican Council, that it looks upon the "world which is the theater of human history and carries the mark of its (i.e. humanity's) energies, tragedies, and triumphs; that world which the Christian sees as created and sustained by its Maker's love, fallen indeed into the bondage of sin, yet emancipated now by Christ. He was crucified and rose again to break the stranglehold of personified evil, so that this world might be fashioned anew according to God's design and reach its fulfillment.''*

A worldview implies the "big picture" or the "long view" of things. If a particular religious tradition it means that, to one degree or another, the communicants of that tradition will share in or be shaped by that worldview. That is what we mean when we say that to be a Catholic is to be in the world in a certain way. It is like the distinction between defining love and being in love. A Catholic does not merely assent to a number of religious propositions (e.g. I believe this; I believe that, etc.) but so sees the world that the way the world looks and the way one looks at the world are distinctive ways of seeing and knowing. The Catholic who sees with the Catholic worldview understands the world as a reflection, however imprecise, of the reality of God; the Catholic sees in human gestures the breakthrough of the divine; the Catholic understands that God speaks to us in palpable and tactile ways. The Catholic, in short, is a sacramentalist.

The Catholic lives in the real tactile world of history but affirms Someone who is prior to, beneath, above, in front of, beyond, and within (all these words are pertinent) this world. That creates a whole series of tensions and paradoxes. Catholics are called upon to live in the world and help in its transformations but not to be immersed in it or see it as being "all there is." Catholics are called upon to sanctify this moment but to also live for the future. They are to affirm life but have no fear of death. They come to understand that the world reflects both the goodness of God and the reality of sin. The Catholic, in short, lives in this world with a certain number of tensions which are never resolved but fully recognized. It is that balancing act which gives the Catholic sense of being in the world both its piquancy and its charm.

Finally, we come to the adjective *Catholic* since we describe our religious community of belief as a Catholic one. What do we mean by that word? In common parlance everyone knows what a Catholic is: a Catholic is not a Protestant. At that level we all understand when reporters speak of the "Catholic vote" just as we understand the sentence, "Catholics play bingo and say the rosary." That use of the term

---

*"The Pastoral Constitution on the Church in the Modern World," in *The Documents of Vatican II*, ed. Abbott *et al.* (New York: Guild, 1966), p. 200. All further citations from the Second Vatican Council are taken from this edition.

is helpful only as a broadly vulgar sociological description which serves its own purposes, but it does not provide us with a good deal of insight.

In the course of this book we will use the word Catholic to mean one of two things: as a description of an identifiable part of the Christian tradition and as the statement of an ideal.

Descriptively speaking, Catholics are those Christians who accept the primacy of the bishop of Rome over the Church (which distinguishes them from the Orthodox and the Anglicans) while emphasizing the sacramental, iconic, and communitarian aspects of Christianity (which distinguishes them from the other churches of the Reformation). It has been customary in recent times to refer to such Christians as Roman Catholics to distinguish them from groups like the Orthodox and Anglicans who also claim continuity with the pre-Reformation Church.

As an ideal, Catholic (the word *catholic* etymologically means "universal") means a search for that universality which Christ demands of his Church. When we say in the creeds that we believe in the "one, holy, catholic, and apostolic" Church, we mean by the phrase "catholic" that we affirm a Church which preaches Christ to the entire world. Catholicism in that sense means that the Church and the Gospel cannot be made a prisoner of a particular language, culture, or race or nation. A person who is a Roman Catholic may take genuine pride in the role the Church has played in the formation of Western culture but will not identify Western culture with Catholicism. "The Faith is Europe; Europe is the Faith" (H. Belloc) has a nice ring to it but it is a very bad miscasting of what Catholicism should be ideally about. In fact—and this is a vividly actual problem for the contemporary Church—serious persons in the Church are trying to understand what it means to be an African or an Asian or a Latin American Catholic in a way that would be true to the spirit of the Gospel, just to the culture of its own place, and not subservient to the inherited modes of thought peculiar to the culture of Europe.

To be truly Catholic means—as the Second Vatican Council insisted over and again—to be open to every impulse of grace which is to be found in the world. To be Catholic is to be open to other cultures, other experiences, and other religious traditions. Like Chaucer's young scholar, a truly Catholic Church is pleased not only to teach but to learn. To be truly Catholic, then, means to listen to the world in which we live. That task of listening is not restricted to religious conversations between believers. To be truly Catholic is to be part of that great human dialogue which, thanks to contemporary communications and the urgent need for peace in the world, is not only desirable but imperative. The Catholic Church has something to say to the world and something to learn from it. It is for that reason that the participants in the Second Vatican Council addressed one of their major documents (on the Church in the modern world) not only to the Church but to all people of good will.

Some Procedures

In the pages of this book we hope to describe the Church not as a body of ideas or a set of beliefs but as a lived experience. The problem with that procedure is that the author writes from the vantage point of his own experience. He cannot speak with authority about the contemplative life of the nun because he is not a nun, just as he cannot speak about the Catholic life of a Latin American or a Pole or an Oriental because his experiences are North American and middle class. His Catholicism also straddles the experiences of both the Church before and after the revolutions of the Second Vatican Council. The author's experiences, in short, are very much his own. Others may have (indeed, will have) other experiences of the Church or, perhaps, no experiences at all.

How do we bridge the gap between the perceptions of the author and those of the putative reader? How do we account for the inevitable fact that certain things about the Church might seem obvious to the writer but strange to the reader? A few strategies to enrich the experience of reading this book might be in order.

Let us assume that the reader is interested in learning more about the Catholic Church. One can learn more by reading this little book but the experience of reading it can be strengthened by doing some other things that provide context and background for our study:

- Read the Bible. It would be most helpful to take the Bible (any standard translation will do) and read, first of all, the narrative story from the ancient patriarchs of the Old Testament through the Gospel story of Jesus. Then one can go back and read the non-narrative parts (e.g. the psalms; the prophets) for further enrichment. My suggestion would be to read the historical narratives without the use of a commentary just to hear the story afresh. After that exercise one can go back to "study" the text. The first task should be, however, that of basic familiarity. Only after one gets a basic familiarity with the "old story" does the reading of the Scriptures in the liturgy begin to make any kind of sense.

- Attend the liturgy. If one *attends,* i.e. really *listens* to the liturgy, much of what is central to the experience of being a Catholic becomes clearer. There is an old saying in the Church that the worship of the Church is its act of faith (*lex orandi lex credendi* is the Latin phrase), and that is surely true.

  Catholic readers might object that they have attended the liturgy all of their lives and, as a consequence, they are familiar with the liturgy to the point of boredom. To those people we can only say that they must relearn the art of listening and seeing. One useful strategy might be to go to the liturgy on a weekday when the liturgy is less formal and more intimate. The relative newness of that experience might yield greater insight. Those who are not familiar with the Catholic liturgy should just take a deep breath and go to church. They will be welcome and very shortly accustomed to what is going on.

- Approach this study with a certain sense of leisure and wonder. We have a very short attention span today. Religion, however, is not like a rock video: it cannot be grasped at the surface in a span of two minutes. By its nature, religion looks beneath, behind, and beyond the surfaces. It requires a certain willingness to stop and look and listen. I hesitate to recommend to the reader that this subject be approached prayerfully (such advice sounds unctuous and pompous), but I would suggest that, if one wants more than just information and facts, it is better to go slowly and with a certain openness. The late John Cogley once wrote that religion, like Scotch whiskey, is an acquired taste. The cultivation of taste takes time and a spirit of adventurousness.

- As an addendum to the above point it might be useful to keep a notebook if only to jot down ideas, questions, disagreements, random thoughts, and so on. The very act of stopping and writing something down is an effective brake on the impulse to rush to get an assignment out of the way or a chore finished. In short, it helps to lengthen the attention span.

A final observation: this is not a book on spirituality, but the focus and bias of this book moves strongly in that direction. This book will try, to the extent that it is possible, to describe Catholicism as an experience of faith and as an adventure (or pilgrimage or journey) in belief. For that reason I will not hesitate, where useful, to make use of the life experiences of the great saints, writers, mystics, theologians, and artists of the Catholic tradition. That will be done for two reasons. First, they are the best witnesses to the vitality of the tradition of Catholicism. Second, their mention might tempt the reader to pursue their *personae* in greater depth. They, after all, are the vehicle for keeping the tradition vibrantly alive.

In subsequent chapters I will append a few brief questions or "thought experiments" to allow the interested reader to move beyond the material of the chapter for deeper exploration. No one more than the author understands that this book is a mere sketch; it needs to be filled in, amplified, explored. I will recall here a Zen proverb which I find helpful when reading any book: when a finger is pointed, look not at the finger but in the direction to which it points. This book is very much a first probe; the questions at the end of the chapters are meant to expand the skirmish lines a bit.

Chapter II

The Word of God
to His People

The simplest way to learn about the Catholic Church is to see it in action. There is no better way of doing that than to go to a typical Catholic parish for Mass on Sunday. I have often told my students that one could get a firm grasp on Catholicism by a careful study of a typical parish "plant" in Anywhere, USA. The architecture, the decoration, the buildings, the shape of the liturgy, the clergy, religious, and laity, the behavior of the congregation—all of those observable phenomena have a long history behind them. To see these phenomena and to understand how they got there and why they are there is to receive a compressed history of the Church.

For the present we shall simply focus on the celebration of the Mass. Since that celebration is now in the vernacular (the use of Latin was typical until a generation ago) we can hear the liturgy in a form that is at least minimally intelligible. If we listen clearly to the liturgy at our hypothetical Mass one fact becomes abundantly obvious: the liturgy is saturated in the language of the Bible, and the actual texts of the Bible have an honored place in the celebration. The first part of the liturgy (up through the sermon or homily) centers on three readings from the Bible introduced by a prayer and interspersed with short responses which are also culled from the Bible. Typically those three readings are taken, in order, from the Hebrew Scriptures, the writings of Paul, and, finally, one of the four Gospels. In the second part of the liturgy the language of the Bible saturates the prayers and proclamations.

We should further note as we listen that the Bible is used in different ways in the liturgy. There are the readings to which we alluded above. There are prayers taken directly from places like the Book of Psalms or from the Gospels (e.g. the Lord's Prayer). The one sure conclusion that we can deduce from this first observation is that the Bible is a critical and shaping force at the very center of Catholic worship. That seems so obvious that we may well begin our discussion with the issue of the Catholic attitude toward the Bible. We might begin this discussion by keeping in the back of our mind the way the Bible is used in the liturgy: as a source of instruction and as a source of piety and worship and as a standard of what we profess as believers.

Before we begin our discussion in depth it might be well to set out a general and authoritative statement of what the Catholic Church believes about the Bible in general. Here is the statement of the Second Vatican Council in its Dogmatic Constitution on Divine Revelation:

> Holy Mother Church, relying on the belief of the apostles, holds that the books of the Old and New Testament in their entirety, with all their parts, are sacred and canonical because, having been written under the inspiration of the Holy Spirit, they have God as their author and have been handed on as such to the church herself.*

The Old Testament

The Old Testament is a story, a promise, and a prayer. It is not a book but many books.

If one were to puzzle out the narrative thread of the Old Testament (not an easy task since the books are not in strict chronological order and some of them have no narrative) the story would follow this general line: God calls a man named Abraham from Ur of the Chaldees in order to be the father of his people. Abraham and his descendants (the so-called patriarchs) were wandering herdsmen who regarded their God as uniquely God and themselves as his unique people. These people were eventually enslaved in Egypt where they lived as forced laborers working on the great projects of the pharaohs. Their deliverance came under the leadership of Moses who was called by God to take the people out of Egypt. He led the Israelites out of Egypt into the desert of the Sinai peninsula where God revealed to them his law. After the death of Moses the people of Israel slowly penetrated, and finally subdued, the land which was promised to them. When they had hold of the land they desired a king. The monarchy of Israel lasted for three generations: from Saul to David to Solomon. After the death of Solomon the kingdom was torn by civil strife and eventually divided in two kingdoms, with Israel to the north and Judah, with its capital Jerusalem, to the south. These small and militarily weak kingdoms were easy prey for their more powerful neighbors. The northern kingdom first fell, and then, in 587 B.C., Jerusalem and the kingdom of Judah fell to the Babylonians who carried the Jews into captivity. The temple of Solomon was destroyed and the

---

*The Dogmatic Constitution on Divine Revelation, III. 11, in Documents, p. 118.

Jews did not reenter their land until seventy years later. From that time of the rebuilding of the temple until the time of Jesus the Jews lived in Israel (although many lived in other parts of the world; they were known as the diaspora), but under a series of despotic powers, including the Persians and the Greeks, until Rome finally made Israel one of its many dependent colonies.

In the liturgy of the Catholic Church that story is told through a cycle of readings which extends over a cycle of years. It should be obvious, however, that this "retelling" is not done in order to keep alive ancient historical sagas which happened millennia ago. In fact, that story is told and retold because the Catholic Church believes that God intervened in history in a decisive way in those events by choosing a specific people who would be the vehicle of his concern for the world.

What is the character of that intervention and that concern? It seems presumptuous to attempt a summary of the complex riches of the Hebrew Scriptures in a few pages, but we can outline, at least, some of the salient elements which are crucial for an understanding of this story for the faith and life of the Catholic faith. We shall set these elements out in serial fashion since they are crucial for our whole discussion.

(1) The God of Israel is not an impersonal principle or a provincial tyrant. The God of Israel was not a product of creation or identified with creation itself. The God of the Bible is the God of history and the Lord of the world. Yet that God interacts with the world in general and the people of Israel in an intimate fashion. That interaction is best summed up by the word *covenant,* and that covenant is, in turn, summed up by the phrase: "I will be your God and you will be my people." Many scholars have noted that the language of the covenant between God and his people is borrowed from the language of ancient marriage covenants (e.g. "She is my wife and I am her husband") in common use in the Middle East. The implication of that fact is clear: the relationship of God and the people he chose is as intimate as the relationship of spouses. In fact, the image of God as the spouse of Israel is a common one in the Bible.

(2) The events of Israel's history were not random events of mere social forces. For the Bible, history is a reflection of the great things that God has done for Israel. The biblical authors make constant reference to the shaping and guiding hand of God as the events of history unfold. In ancient prayers like Psalm 136 God's goodness is praised not only for his gift of creation but because God also brought the children

of Israel out of a land of slavery, gave them a land to dwell in, and watches over that same people even when they are in a "low estate" or in the hands of their foes (Ps 136:23–24). God, in brief, is a providential ruler of his chosen people.

(3) The response of Israel, like all human responses, was not always faithful to the concerns of God. Israel could stray from the covenant, but God, like a faithful spouse, would call Israel back to fidelity. The great agent of that recall was the prophet. Called by God, the prophet spoke in God's name to excoriate infidelity and to recall God's graciousness and fidelity to the covenant. The prophetic message insisted that God was not satisfied with external obedience; God wanted a pure heart and a changed person. The prophets also insisted that conversion to God was a mockery if it did not also include a concern for God's creation, especially those who were most vulnerable in the world: the poor and oppressed. The great prophet Amos, for example, has God say that solemn religious assemblies do not please nor are sacrifices acceptable nor are the hymns to God heard unless "justice rolls down like waters, and righteousness like an everlasting stream" (cf. Am 5:21–24). There is, as seems obvious from that passage, an intimate nexus between religious fidelity and ethical action; neither can exist without the other.

(4) The history of Israel has a strong orientation toward the future. In the early period of the patriarchs—Abraham, Isaac, Jacob—there were promises made to Abraham concerning the future. God tells Abraham that he will father a "great nation" (Gen 12:2), while Isaac is promised a country for his descendants and "by your descendants all the nations of the earth shall bless themselves" (Gen 26:4). To Isaac's son Jacob similar blessings were repeated (cf. Gen 28:1–4).

(5) Out of these promises and from the covenantal relationship there evolved the conviction that God would extend his reign in a more universal manner so that God would rule the world in peace and justice. This universal reign would be heralded by a *Messiah*, i.e. one who was anointed of God. This Messiah would appear in God's good time to reaffirm the covenant in strength and bring to the world peace and justice.

Christians, of course, have affirmed that Jesus of Nazareth is that one who was promised. Before we press that point, however, there are a number of observations to be made. The first is that Christianity is absolutely unintelligible except against the background of Jewish history and the Hebrew Scriptures. The point is obvious, but let us insist on it. When Catholics go to Mass on Sunday the first thing they hear proclaimed are the Hebrew Scriptures, while many of the prayers they use are Hebrew prayers. The Book of Psalms is often called the Church's prayerbook, but one must remember that long before there was a Church it was the prayerbook of both the temple and the synagogue.

The essential difference between the Hebrew and Christian reading of the Bible is that the Christian Church reads the Hebrew Bible both for its own revelatory power *and* as a revelation that points inexorably to Jesus the Christ. This Christian approach to the Bible is encapsulated in a famous strophe from the Epistle to the Hebrews in the New Testament:

> In many and various ways God spoke of old to our fathers by the prophets; but in these last days he has spoken to us by a Son, whom he appointed the heir to all things and through whom he also created the world. He reflects the glory of God and bears the very stamp of his nature, upholding the universe by his word of power (Heb 1:1–3).

The fact that Christianity reads back into the Hebrew Scriptures to find Christ results in a rather complex set of understandings which the Church has adopted over the centuries. Apart from the historical/critical study of the Scriptures, there is yet another general way in which the Scriptures are studied and/or understood within the Church. Without getting into the very complex (but fascinating) topic of how the Bible is read in its various "senses," we can set down as a generalization a principle which informs the understanding of the Scriptures as they are utilized in the proclamations of the liturgy. It runs something like this: when we hear the Hebrew Scriptures in church we first hear them as a revelation in themselves. When we listen to the Old Testament readings we affirm the majesty of God in Israel's language, we accept the ethical demands of things like the ten commandments, and we try to conform to those conversions of heart demanded by the prophets. To make the point concretely: when the prophet Amos demands that justice roll down like running waters, that demand is as urgent today as it was for the first audience of Amos or for our Jewish neighbors today who hear that same passage read aloud in the synagogue. What is added for the Christian hearer is the answer to this query: In what manner does Jesus aid in the doing of the justice demanded by Amos? At that level we read back into the message of the Old Testament our experience in faith of Jesus the Christ.

There is as yet another second level by which we read the Scriptures. The Christian Church sees in the lived events of the Hebrew people interventions of a living God which were interventions for that people and a sign-promise for Christianity. We can make that level of understanding clearer by looking at the event which next to the covenant was the most important moment in Israel's history: the exodus from the land of Egypt and its bondage and the subsequent entry into the promised land.

The exodus is connected with the story of Moses, the plagues of Egypt, the Passover meal, the going out into the desert, the reception of the law at Sinai and the covenant, and the entry into the promised land. The exodus is at the very heart of the Jewish experience and its remembrance is crucial for the memory and maintenance of the people of Israel. Every year at Passover the exodus story is retold in the context of a meal which memorializes the last one that the Jews ate before their departure. That meal together with the recital of the exodus events has been a part of Jewish life for millennia. I have often told my students that there is no way they can appreciate the Jewish love for Israel unless they remember that for centuries Jews have said with all solemnity at that annual meal: "Next year in Jerusalem!"

It is hard to overestimate the impact of that great biblical story on the shape of Christianity.* In the New Testament Paul sees the passage of the children of Israel through the Red Sea as a foreshadowing of baptism and the manna in the desert as an anticipation of the presence of Christ (cf. 1 Cor 10). The point is that what is in the Old Testament has its own integrity but is also a foreshadowing of the reality of Jesus. It is for that reason that Paul insists on the uniqueness of Israel's role in the formation of the Christian faith:

> To them belong the sonship, the glory, the covenants, the giving of the law, the worship, and the promises; to them belong the patriarchs, and of their race, according to the flesh, is the Christ (Rom 9:4–5).

---

*The power of that story in political liberation has been brilliantly studied in Michael Walzer's *Exodus and Revolution* (New York: Basic Books, 1985).

The New Testament

The very term "New Testament" tells us a great deal about the connection between Judaism and Christianity. Testament translates the Greek word *diatheke* which in the Bible means, simply, covenant. Thus, one could call the Christian scriptures the new covenant since one of its claims is that the covenant between God and his people is made anew in the person and work of Jesus.

At every Catholic liturgy a selection from St. Paul (or from one of the other letters) is read and, following on that, a selection from one of the four Gospels is proclaimed by the priest. Ordinarily the priest will then speak on the Scripture readings of the day. The New Testament is so central to the Church's proclamations—as the liturgy makes clear—that we will make constant references to it throughout our work. At this juncture it is only necessary to say a few words about the use of the term "word of God" when we refer to the New Testament and the Old Testament.

When we say that the Bible is the word of God it should be first stated that the Church never understood by this that God dropped a book into the midst of the world as a finished literary product. Nor does the Church think that certain writers took down word for word dictation from God as a stenographer might do. As many of the separate works in the New Testament clearly indicate, much of the New Testament was written in the early Church to meet specific and urgent needs. Furthermore, there are places in the New Testament where the writers tell us quite explicitly that a particular work was written in order to strengthen the faith of the early followers of Jesus. Thus, Luke, at the beginning of his Gospel (Gospel means "good news"), says that he wrote his work so that its recipient, a person called Theophilus, "may know the truth of the things of which you have been informed" (Lk 1:4). John, at the end of his Gospel, says that Jesus did many other things which are not recorded in his work but he recorded signs so that "you may believe Jesus is the Christ, the Son of God, and that believing you might have life in his name" (Jn 20:30).

The Catholic Church accepts the Scriptures as the word of God but sees the Scriptures within the context of the living Church which produced the Scriptures, accepted those which it considers inspired of God, and serves as a protector of their integrity. The word of God is a revelation of God's dealing with humanity. The Church accepts the notion—indeed, it teaches it—that God speaks in a unique and special way in the Scriptures. For that reason the Church is "not above the word of God, but serves it, teaching only what has been handed on, listening to it devoutly, guarding it scrupulously, and explaining it faithfully by divine commission and with the help of the Holy Spirit."*

Catholics believe that when the Scriptures are proclaimed in church, that is not only the correct place to hear the Scriptures but in that proclamation we are listening to the word of God.

As we listen to that proclamation, what do we hear of Jesus the Christ? To answer that question adequately would require encyclopedias. At this stage of our exploration we must satisfy ourselves with a few preliminary observations and some first reflections. Since, as we have said, Jesus is at the center of the Catholic experience, we will turn in detail to the question of Jesus and his meaning throughout this work.

If we would listen faithfully to the whole cycle of readings from the New Testament as they are proclaimed in church at the liturgy, these generalizations would hold:

(1) There is no single portrait or image of Jesus in any one place in the New Testament which does complete justice to the whole. The Jesus of the Gospel of Mark is somewhat different from that of John, just as the epistles of Paul fail to emphasize things found in the Gospel of Luke. It is not a question of contradiction but of complexity, paradox, and mystery. The conclusion that the Church draws from this fact is that we can never fully "explain" or capture the reality of Jesus. Jesus is always a mystery to be approached in the Gospel, not some kind of problem to be solved.

(2) There seem to be at least two angles of vision with respect to the Jesus of the New Testament. One angle focuses on a man who was an artisan's son who trudges through the dust of Galilee and Judea accepting the company of common fishermen, ordinary men and women, and those—like the tax collector and prostitute—who were at the very margins of society. The other angle of vision is far more exalted: Jesus as the Son of God who pre-existed with God from all eternity, through whom the world was created, and who now dwells in eternity at "the right hand of the Father" who will return at the end of time in glory.

Those two angles of vision—what the theologians call, respectively, Christology "from below" and Christology "from above"—

---

*Dogmatic Constitution on Divine Revelation, II. 10, in Documents, p. 118.

are biblical reflections of a deep Christian conviction: that Jesus, truly man, is also divine. Jesus is, as the old formulation would have it, the God Man.

(3) An understanding (or, better, an approach to an understanding) of Jesus will demand that we may make sense of the titles given to Jesus in the New Testament. We must ask: What does it mean to say that Jesus is the Christ? the Son of Man? the Son of God? Lord? son of Mary? Each of these titles—and there are many of them—has a full freight of scriptural tradition behind it as well as a distinct meaning for the Christian community from where the New Testament arose.

(4) It is clear that the New Testament does not regard Jesus as merely an ethical teacher or a miracle worker or a political or religious reformer. Jesus did teach, he did perform miracles, and he had much to say about both social and religious behavior. There is, however, something more, and that "more" is at the very core of what the early New Testament Church believed about Jesus. That "more" is summed up in one of the earliest statements of Christian belief which we possess. Paul recalls for the Church at Corinth the Gospel which he had already preached to them. It was a Gospel, as he says, which he himself had received:

> That Christ died for our sins in accordance with the
> Scriptures,
>> that he was buried,
>> that he was raised on the third day according
> to the Scriptures (1 Cor 15:3–4).

(5) Central to our understanding then is that Jesus died for "our sins" and that God raised him up from the dead. That means that Jesus, according to the faith of the Church, is one who saves us and that the seal of his saving power is founded on the resurrection. Jesus Christ, in short, is not merely a dead martyr or an historical religious founder. Jesus Christ is a *living* Savior. It might be appropriate here to state that the resurrection, in the faith of the Church, is not merely a pure "faith experience" of the early Church. The power and significance of the resurrection is in what happened to Jesus and only then in what happened to his followers. This point is so important that it might be better framed in the words of some professional biblical scholars:

> We can readily admit that the language of the resurrection is derived
> from Jewish apocalyptic and is therefore itself mythological. But it

is the mythological language for something that God did with Jesus, not just for what God did with the disciples. If we want non-mythological language to describe what God did with Jesus at Easter, the best we can say is that God translated Jesus into eschatological existence, into life out of death.*

Within the framework of the death, burial, and resurrection of Christ we begin to understand him (and ourselves in relation to him) in terms beyond that of the great religious teacher. Jesus is proclaimed in the Christian faith as a victor over alienation, sin, and, finally, death itself. In one of the eucharistic prayers of the liturgy this work of Christ and his significance is eloquently proclaimed:

> To the poor he proclaimed the good news of salvation,
> to prisoners, freedom,
> and to those in sorrow, joy.
> In fulfillment of your will
> he gave himself up to death;
> but by his rising from the dead,
> he destroyed death and restored life.**

(6) Despite the exalted claims made for Jesus the risen Christ we must also remember that the New Testament also depicts Jesus as a human being who was, in the words of St. Paul, "born under the law" and "born of a woman" (Gal 4:4). With that brief description Paul reminds us that Jesus was in this world as a real person. He was born into a particular historical and cultural order (i.e. he was a Jew "born under the law") and he was a child of our race "born of a woman."

For the Catholic the humanness of Jesus means that at least once in the long history of humanity someone lived who resolved the terrible ambiguities of human existence. There is one person who can stand as a model, a paradigm, and a standard against which we can take measure of our own lives and toward which we can dare to aspire. The proclamations of the New Testament in the Church's liturgy, then, is not only designed to say out loud that we have been redeemed from sin and death but that there is someone who is present to us who can aid in that long process of becoming more human.

---

*Reginald H. Fuller and Pheme Perkins, *Who Is This Christ? Gospel Christology and Contemporary Faith* (Philadelphia: Fortress, 1983), p. 36.

**Eucharistic Prayer IV.*

As a model, Jesus is not to be thought of—at least if one is attempting to be serious and honest with the Scriptures—as an abstract symbol or metaphor. Jesus is a living model. As a model he shows that our human condition, with all its burdens and glories, can be stretched, deepened, and made over in yet undiscovered ways. Jesus is the pledge that the evils and anxieties which afflict us can be overcome just as the desires which push us toward a fuller life can be attained. In that sense the basic questions which Christianity proposes for consideration is this: Is not humanity better off by the fact that Jesus lived, is remembered, proclaimed, and imitated? The "better-offness" is the clue which permits us to begin to plumb the depth of the significance of Jesus.

That the Church sees continuing relevance in the person of Jesus the Christ explains why the Church insists that every Sunday there should be a homily preached on the significance and applicability of the proclaimed Scriptures. The Scriptures are not merely a record of the past or a memory book of Jesus. We read the text which comes down to us but, in turn, the text also reads us. At least in part the homily functions to provide those explicit links between the text as it is preserved in the worship of the Church and the demands and exigencies of our life today. The homily is the bridge between the reality of God's revelation as it is remembered and our lives of faith as they are lived.

Catholics believe that the word of God is inexhaustible in its richness. It strongly affirms the perennial and relevant power of the Scriptures to speak to each age and to every condition. One fact that emerges from that conviction is that the Church believes that it has never fully grasped or articulated the full meaning of revelation. The Church is a teaching Church but it is also one that learns. It might well be worth remembering that every Sunday people all over the world are listening to the scriptural proclamations in the liturgy. They attempt to reach out to those proclamations to learn and deepen their understanding of God's word to them. From the baroque splendors of the church of St. Peter in the Vatican to the meanest chapel in a *barrio* of Central America the word is preached with certainty and with expectation. We should remember also that this happens not only in our time but has happened for nearly two millennia. To be Catholic means—at least in part—to be in the company of those who stand before the word of God and listen. To be Catholic, in short, is to stand in time and as part of history with those who are prompt to respond to what they hear.

The Many Faces of Christ

The Scriptures are the source and reference point for the Catholic preaching about Jesus the Christ. We must insist again, however, that it is Jesus and not the record of him that is the central subject of Catholic belief. The Catholic Church preaches Christ, not the Scriptures.

We have already said that it is impossible to get a single composite picture of Christ from the Scriptures. If we assume—as we must—that the New Testament is a witness to what the earliest Christian communities believed about Jesus, then we must conclude that the earliest communities already interpreted the significance of Christ in different ways according to different points of view and according to quite different needs. The early community of the New Testament Church could say in faith that "Jesus is Lord" but the word "Lord" might mean quite different things to a Gentile or a Jewish hearer of that proclamation in faith. It might even mean something different to a Jew in Palestine and one in a diaspora community. To proclaim that Jesus was the Word (cf. Jn 1:1) would resonate very differently to a Jew who might think of God's creative word in the creation accounts of Genesis and a Greek who might well think of the technical term *Logos* as it was commonly used in philosophy. The point is this: already in the New Testament people were reaching up to the meaning of the mystery of Jesus and his meaning.

Those attempts, detected in the New Testament itself, to come to grips with the mystery of Jesus fairly well defines the task of the Church as a whole: to preserve and to deepen the revelation of God in Jesus. If the New Testament reveals many facets to the story of Jesus, it should not surprise us that the same is true of the later periods of Church history. As we read in that history we see rather clearly that there were titanic struggles to seek out the meaning of Christ without compromising those elements of his reality which were central to the Christian faith. In the early centuries of the Church there was a great battle about the central issue of the significance of Jesus as both human and divine. We see from the vantage point of time that the Church did not want (and could not tolerate) a Jesus who was some sort of heavenly creature who only *seemed* human. Nor did it want to accept a supremely holy ethical teacher whose only claim to divinity was his relationship to God through piety or faith. The orthodox definitions of Jesus as one who was a single person with the two natures of humanity and divinity was an attempt to somehow articulate a profound mystery in a manner which would safeguard the faith from straying onto paths alien to the apostolic preaching of the New Testament itself.

The immensely complex development of Christology (i.e., the study of Christ) from the New Testament through the controversies of the early centuries and into the Middle Ages and beyond to our own day is one witness to the constant desire of the Church to do two things: (a) to be faithful to the witness of the New Testament, and (b) to deepen our understanding of that witness. In its details that process is too complicated and too technical for consideration in a work of this modest scope. One can get some sense of the evolution and complexity of our understanding of Christ, however, by the very simple expedient of thinking about the ways in which Christ has been portrayed historically in art. Using any standard art history* we would simply look at the illustrations for the chapters on early Christian, Byzantine, medieval, Renaissance, and baroque art. Such a page turning perusal triggers some very interesting observations and some very sharp contrasts.

Every period depicts *its* Christ, and its Christ makes constant reference to the culture in which it is found. The early beardless Christ of Roman Christianity stands in sharp contrast to the fiercely rendered apse mosaics of the Byzantine churches. Those Byzantine pantocrater (lit. "the One who holds all in his hands") figures speak of a Christ who creates, sustains, and rules the world—just the kind of figure one might suspect from a culture where the emperor was a surrogate of God on earth and ruled with absolute power. The great pantocrater figures reflect one understanding of Christ; the suffering crucified Christ of the medieval period reflects another. In the Middle Ages there was a deepened devotion to the passion of Christ, and the suffering Christ became a common way to depict him in art.

The pantocrater tradition put great emphasis on the divinity of Christ; the suffering Christ emphasized his humanity. Another theme, very ancient in the history of art, tried to do justice to both aspects of Christ. From the third century on we have frequent depictions of Mary holding the child on her lap with the child facing out to the viewer. In

---

*I have in mind any of the standard texts: H. W. Janson, *History of Art* (New York: Prentice Hall/Abrahams, 1969); Helen Gardner *et al.*, *Art Through The Ages* (New York: Harcourt Brace, 1970); H. Honour and John Fleming, *The Visual Arts: A History* (Englewood Cliffs: Prentice-Hall, 1982); etc.

the earliest depictions Mary sits on a rather chaste but unmistakable throne. That formal arrangement meant to convey that Mary was the true Mother of God (the *Theotokos*). Mary presents her Son to the world just as the Church would continue to do so. Thus, she is also a *figura* of the Church. But the fact that Jesus had a Mother reminded the viewer that Jesus was part of our common humanity in that he was "born of a woman" (Gal 4:4).

The motif of the Mother and Child is deeply rooted in the Catholic imagination. Indeed, it was commonly said of Catholics that there was an excessive interest in Mary and that interest obscured the uniqueness of Christ. Yet the point to remember is this: the tradition of the Madonna and Child in Christian art is meant to be a forceful reminder that the presence of Christ in the world was a *mediated* one. It was through the consent of Mary that the Savior entered the world. That is why we were able to say above that Mary is a symbol of the Church (we call the Church a mother—*Sancta Mater Ecclesia*—Holy Mother the Church) and the prototype of every Christian. Ideally, both the Church and the individual believer do what Mary first did: consent to the reality of Christ and mediate his presence in the world.

All of these notions—and many others—are embedded in the tradition of Christian art. From the time of the Renaissance on we see the figure of both Christ and his Mother become softened and increasingly humanized in art. From Michelangelo's *Pietá* to the Madonnas of Raphael we see artists attempting to depict perfectly idealized humanity and perfectly realized human emotions like tenderness, love, sorrow, and so on. In baroque painters like Caravaggio Jesus is often depicted in perfectly human settings. Caravaggio's famous "Supper at Emmaus" looks like a scene in an ordinary Roman *trattoria*. One is tempted to see those kinds of representations as a secularizing tendency when, in reality, such humanizing scenes were consistent with the spiritual teaching of Ignatius of Loyola's *Spiritual Exercises* where people were strongly encouraged in their prayer to vividly imagine the scenes of the Gospel as real, vibrant scenes.

Obviously we cannot trace out every motif and nuance of the image of Christ in the history of Western art. What we gave above was only to make a point. When we look at the history of Western art in a roughly chronological fashion we see one unassailable fact: the person of Jesus the Christ is an inexhaustible source for the imagination and piety of a given age. That is true as an historical fact and as an observed reality. Every Sunday, all over the Catholic world, people listen to the Gospel being preached and attempt to make sense of that message according to their needs, their times, their personal and social condition. These "hearers of the word" never fully exhaust the meaning of the Gospel which is set before them. Those who mourn may hear the Christ who comforts; those who are beaten down may hear the Christ who liberates; those who falter find the One who strengthens; those who love find the way to deeper love.

To say that Christ has many faces and many meanings does not mean to imply that there is no deeply real center to the person of Christ. Jesus is not merely passive clay that can be molded or shaped into any form without reference to limits. Jesus is not Proteus who can take any shape. The very fact that the Scriptures are the Church's book, born of its faith and guarded by the community, means that some interpretations are not acceptable. The Christian community's tradition always seeks new understandings and insights into the person of Christ but it jealously resists any understanding which is alien to its own sense of faithfulness to the Gospel. The conservative character of tradition helps us to avoid the enthusiasms of the present age and their deformities. Tradition is both a check against deformity and an act of faith in the vitality of the Christian message.

Some years ago I saw a poster for sale which showed Christ with a bandolier of cartridges over his shoulder and his right arm raised clenching an automatic weapon. Under the picture was the word "Venceremos"—"We shall prevail!" However well-meaning the sentiment was to enlist Jesus into the cause of revolutionary politics it is a false and pernicious view of the Gospel. Despite the number of wars fought under the banner of Christianity, neither the New Testament nor the worshiping community allows for an armed Christ who kills for the sake of a cause. The notion of an armed and warring Christ is alien to everything we find in the New Testament understanding of Christ. It is a deformation not because it trivializes the person of Christ (as does, for example, a rock opera like *Jesus Christ Superstar*) but because it subverts the very meaning of Jesus. As Walter Kasper has noted, the authentic Jesus of the New Testament extended love and friendship not only to the poor and oppressed but to those who oppress or who are in the oppressing class. Kasper writes:

Jesus' behavior in this regard drew attention and even aroused anger, but how little it had to do with what is normally thought of today as social concern or revolution can be seen from the fact that the tax collectors were in no sense the exploited, but the exploiters, who collaborated with the Roman occupying power. Jesus had come for them too; his message of God's love was also for them. . . . God is a God for all people, people of all sorts, and his commandments exist for the sake of people.*

Remember the old theological proverb: *lex orandi, lex credendi* (the rule of worship is the rule of faith). It is so easy to forget that one of the first ways that we discover the complexity—the many faces of—Christ is in the worship of the Christian Church. Orthodoxy, after all, means not correct doctrine, but correct praise or worship. In the formal witness of the liturgy we see many sides of Christ as he is invoked both by title (Son, Lamb, King, etc.) and by way of our prayerful approach: as object of worship, as respondent to petitions, as giver of forgiveness, as sustainer of our hopes, etc. All of these words and gestures—once we begin to reflect on them—testify to the riches hidden in the person and words of the Christ of the Gospel.

It is obvious that not all of our understandings of Christ come from worship. We learn of Christ both in our own experience in faith and through the example of those who have encountered him in prayer and living (the mystics, saints, spiritual mothers and fathers of our tradition) and through the reflective efforts of our theologians and the imaginative work of our artists. In all of these cases we ask a simple and direct series of questions: Does this or that depiction resonate with the historical witness of the Church? Does it add to my understanding? Is it a worthy addition to that great line of those who have responded to Christ in time and space? In all of those efforts we detect the complex reality of Christ. We see the truth of the observation of the great nineteenth century poet priest, Gerard Manley Hopkins:

> For Christ plays in ten thousand places,
> Lovely in limbs, and lovely in eyes not his
> To the Father through the feature of men's faces.

---

*Walter Kasper, *Jesus the Christ* (New York: Paulist, 1977), p. 67.

Points for Discussion

(a) Are there images, persons, stories, or symbols from the Scriptures which have a deep hold on your imagination? What do they say? Where did you encounter them?

(b) If you were to describe "your" Christ to another person what would be his most salient features? What would he look like? Where in the Scriptures would you go to find a description of "your" Christ?

(c) When, if ever, have the words of the Scriptures touched you most directly when you have heard them in the liturgy?

(d) What do you think is the biggest obstacle to hearing the word of God in worship today? What would you propose to do about that obstacle?

(e) What about the Scriptures do you see as foreign to you? What would you most like to learn about with respect to Scripture study and how do you think you could go about learning?

Chapter III

The Eucharist in Life

If we once again imagine ourselves at our hypothetical Sunday liturgy and are still attentive to what is going on (not easy since it took me a whole chapter just to talk about the scriptural proclamations which take up the first few minutes of the service), we will notice that after the homily is preached there is a decided shift in the service from *saying* to *doing*. Gifts are brought to the altar (bread, wine, water, and the Sunday collection) and presented to the priest. The priest makes an offering of these gifts and then prepares for the central prayer of the liturgy. The great solemn eucharistic prayer (the word "eucharist" means thanksgiving) is said aloud; the Lord's Prayer is recited in unison; people come forward to share in the consecrated bread and wine; an interlude of silence is observed after which the officiating priest announces the end of the celebration. The formal Sunday liturgy is completed.

This act of "doing" is the second part of the liturgy and the natural complement to the first part of "saying." The two parts are often called the "liturgy of the word" and the "liturgy of the faithful" or the "liturgy of the Eucharist." For now I want to underscore that this second part of the liturgy has, for all of its ritual formality, the character of a *meal*. This meal has a very stylized and sacred character to it, so we might begin by inquiring about its basic significance.

Let us begin with a few words which St. Paul once wrote to the church at Corinth:

> For I also received from the Lord what I delivered to you, that the Lord Jesus on the night he was betrayed took bread and when he had given thanks, he broke it and said: "This is my body which is for you. Do this in remembrance of me." In the same manner also the cup, after supper, saying, "This cup is the new covenant in my blood. Do this, as often as you drink it, in remembrance of me." For as often as you eat this bread and drink the cup, you proclaim the Lord's death until he comes (1 Cor 11:23–26).

There are a number of things to note about that crucial passage in St. Paul. First, Paul reminds the church at Corinth that he is handing on a tradition which he had received from Jesus. Second, Paul notes

41

that the essential elements of this ritual meal were as Jesus celebrated them "on the night before he died." That ritual was so central to the early faith that it is elsewhere described in the New Testament (in the Gospels of Mark, Matthew, and Luke) albeit in somewhat different words. Finally, Paul not only recalls what Jesus did and orders it to be repeated but gives a rationale for that repetition: it recalls the death of Jesus, and that recollection is to be a constant in the life of the community until, as Paul says, the Lord comes again at the end of history.

The ritual meal of Jesus was—let it be emphasized one more time—a *meal*. In the Jewish milieu of Jesus a meal in which the head of the table blessed the elements of that meal was a festive commonplace. It symbolized unity in the family, fellowship, a celebration, a common bond, and, finally, it was an act of worship. Jesus, then, took an ancient ritual (the Passover meal) and provided it with a new and rather specific meaning suited to his message. Hans Küng has stated that meaning forcefully:

> In the face of his imminent death he interpreted bread and wine—
> so to speak—as prophetic signs of his death and thus of all that he
> was, did, and willed: of the sacrifice, of the surrender of his life.
> Like this bread, so would his body be broken; like the red wine, so
> would his blood be poured out: this is my body, my blood. In both
> cases what is meant is the whole person and his sacrifice, whole
> and entirely.*

It is out of that moment, ritualized in the active worship of the ancient Christian community, that the central act of Christian worship, called variously the liturgy, the Mass, the Eucharist, developed. Over the course of many centuries the simple meal of Jesus took on a whole freight of ritualized gesture and symbol so that for the uninitiated a solemn service like the papal liturgy in Rome or a Byzantine liturgy in an Eastern church seems a far cry from the spare description of the Eucharist as we have it recorded in the New Testament.

We shall not attempt to trace the complex development of the liturgy here, but there is one thing we should note at least in passing: the tendency of the Catholic Church to invest its life with formal symbolic gestures and rituals. That tendency is one more reminder of a point which will be made often in these pages: the Catholic Church not only

---

*Hans Küng, *On Being a Christian* (Garden City: Doubleday, 1976), p. 324.

has a tendency to use a gesture, but once it begins to use it, it "remembers" it in its tradition. It becomes part of the Church's collective memory. In the light of that fact we can say that many of the formalities of our present day liturgy testify to a very long evolution. The bows, the gestures, the vestments, the rhythm of the service, and so on all have entered into the liturgy at specific moments and have been integrated into the pattern of things. One could see the present liturgy as a sort of summary of much of the Church's history.

At this juncture, however, we should stay with the question of meaning. What does this ritual meal, celebrated in the form of our present day liturgy, mean? We shall answer that question, which is a highly complex one, by treating four interrelated issues. As a summary we can say that the Eucharist must be understood (a) as a meal and (b) as related to the saving death of Jesus and (c) as it relates to the presence of Christ not only as an historical memory but as a here and now reality and (d) as having something to do with the "not yet"—the future. A few words about each.

The Eucharist is a meal. When we have a meal (as opposed to "grabbing a bite to eat") we are almost always in a stylized mode of doing things. We sit down at a determined time with someone at the head of the table; we pass and share dishes; we "mind our manners"; we generally observe a sense of decorum. On festive occasions like Thanksgiving and Christmas we take great pains to make the meal a success and avoid doing anything that would spoil the event. All of us remember parents giving us solemn warnings to be nice to relatives and friends whom in reality, we cannot bear. To eat a meal is a sign of unity, reconciliation, sharing, communication, fellowship, and, to varying degrees, formality. Even our evening meals each day at home, if we think about it for a moment, are ritual moments full of half-articulated significance.

We can carry over to the liturgy some of these same observations. When a Christian community gathers for its weekly worship at the liturgy it celebrates, in the form of a meal, its basic unity. At the beginning of that period we ask God to forgive us our sins; before the Communion we make gestures of unity and peace; we pray and worship together in a set series of gestures. A typical contemporary parish is a complex mixture of young and old, poor and rich, educated and not educated, men and women, liberal and conservative. Even in a fairly homogeneous parish there is a wide variety of needs both physical and moral. In the sharing of the eucharistic meal—at least for that fragile moment—those differences and tensions are subsumed under the more general impulse of a united faith in Christ. At that symbolic level we say as a community that we are in communion with each other and in unity with Christ. That is why it has been a commonplace to say that the local community at worship is a microcosm of what the entire Church should be: a bonded community focused on the central fact of Christ living and triumphant among us.

If the Eucharist were only a fellowship meal, however, it would not be much more significant than those many meals which we have attended as visible signs of our membership in a family or a social group. In the little rural village where I once lived it was a common experience to "pull the community together" with a huge potluck dinner and fishfry. We did that to raise money for a tragedy-struck family or for the volunteer fire department or to express some other form of human and social solidarity. Everyone knows that experience in one form or another. We all recognize, even if implicitly, the deep relation that exists between sharing food and community.*

A close reading of the relevant New Testament passages makes clear that the shared supper of Jesus was more than a sign of social unity. Jesus saw that meal as related to his death in some mysterious fashion. In both Matthew and Mark's account of the Last Supper Jesus sees the cup of wine as his own blood which is "poured out for many for the forgiveness of sins" (cf. Mt 26:28), while St. Paul, in the text quoted earlier in this chapter, says that to celebrate the Eucharist is to announce the death of the Lord until he comes again (cf. 1 Cor 11:26).

What are we to make of this? Clearly, as Hans Küng has noted, the ideas of breaking bread and pouring out wine were seen as vivid symbols of his own violent death and, as such, served the prophetic purpose of Jesus. The Gospel accounts make it clear that Jesus expected this to be a *last* supper: "Truly, I say to you, I shall not drink again of the fruit of the vine until that day when I drink it new in the kingdom of God" (Mk 14:25).

In the course of the centuries theologians and Church teaching had to refine and systematize its understanding of this relationship between the Eucharist and the saving death of Jesus on the cross. Slowly the

---

*Note, for example, that the word *companion* comes from the Latin words *cum* (with) and *panis* (bread); a companion is a "breadsharer."

Church began to articulate the notion that the eucharistic meal is a *sacrifice*. In the sixteenth century the Council of Trent taught that the Eucharist was a "visible sacrifice (as human nature requires), in which that bloody sacrifice, that was once offered on the cross, is made present (*representetur*), preserves his memory until the end of time, and applies his healing power for the forgiveness of sins which we commit on a daily basis."*

About the formulation at the Council of Trent there have swirled many controversies both from Protestants who see such an understanding as denigrating the unique saving event of the cross and from those Catholics who think that there has been too much emphasis on the Mass as sacrifice and not enough on the Mass as a shared meal in worship. Those controversies need not detain us here. For our purposes we can simply state that, at bottom, what the Church is groping for is a way to link the saving death of Christ with those of us who live nearly two millennia after that critical event in history. The Church teaches, in essence, that the unique saving act of Jesus who died for our sins is re-presented, re-enacted, and remembered in every celebration of the liturgy. Catholics accept in faith that there is some deep "making present" of that once and forever act on the cross of Calvary and that "making present" happens in the liturgy. In the *sign* (i.e. the sacrament) of the eucharistic meal the saving work of Christ is made present to us in time and space.

This "re-presentation" is intimately tied to the Catholic belief that Jesus is truly and really present in the Eucharist. When we say "truly" and "really," we do not mean that in some vaporous fashion by which Christ is here as a memory or as a kind of sentimentalized presence as of a dead loved one. The very addition of the term "truly" and "really" to the word "present" is a sign that the Catholic tradition understands this presence in a very specific and special manner. That presence, of course, is linked to religious mystery and is generally called a "sacramental presence." In the high Middle Ages theologians began to use the term *transubstantiation* to speak of that presence, and in the sixteenth century the Council of Trent taught that that term was the most useful way of understanding it. That rather forbidding technical term simply means that the substance of the bread and wine (that reality by

---

*Denziger-Schonemetzer, *Enchiridion Symbolorum* (Herder: Rome, 1976), 1740. My translation.

which it is rightfully called bread and wine) is replaced by the living presence of Christ while the accidental qualities of bread and wine (e.g. texture, color, appearance, etc.) remain.

Whether that understanding of the presence of Jesus in the Eucharist is really helpful today (some theologians think it is not but Church authority has defended it and are reluctant to see it tampered with) depends a great deal on how much sense this approach to philosophical description makes. What is absolutely crucial, however, is that the constant tradition of the Catholic Church teaches us that in the liturgy Christ is among us and in the eucharistic elements themselves Christ is truly and really present. Like the apostles on the road to Emmaus (cf. Lk 24:13ff) we recognize Jesus in "the breaking of bread." In a manner quite distinct from our faith experiences in prayer, Scripture reading, and devotion we find Jesus most vividly in the Eucharist. The real presence of Christ in the Eucharist is a sign (a *sacramentum*) that Jesus is still present with us, that he intrudes into our history, that he makes his presence felt "among us," that he is a living pledge of our faith.

St. Paul writes to the church at Corinth that this celebration of the Eucharist should be done "until he comes again." At the end of history the Eucharist will give way to the reign of Jesus as Lord of history. The Eucharist is the sign and presence of Jesus as he touches us "between the times"—i.e. between his earthly life and the end of history. In the celebration of and communion with Jesus in the Eucharist we express our faith in the Jesus both of past history and of future promise. The crucial element of futurity is basic to the New Testament's understanding of the Eucharist. It would be worthwhile to read the great final discourse of Jesus in John's Gospel to see this in specific detail. In those great chapters (13–17) Jesus, in the context of the Last Supper, treats at great length his continuing presence in the world, the promise of the Holy Spirit, and the intimate relationship of himself to the Father which is a mirror image of our relationship to him.

If we wish to summarize what we have said to this point it might be phrased something like this: the Eucharist is a communal ritual meal which testifies to and signifies the bond of unity between Jesus and the believing community; in that common celebration of faith the presence of Jesus is affirmed as real, his presence celebrated, his power over sin acknowledged, and the hope for the future expressed. We can make our own the words of the theologian James Mackey:

It is because our Eucharists ritually make us one body with the man who celebrated life in death, who made death itself stamp with the seal of its awful finality, the authenticity of his lived conviction that all life was God's gift and not human property. It is because of this that these Eucharists are memorials of the death of Jesus—not because a sacrament has some magic by which, in defiance of finite time systems, it can make present today an ancient tragedy which took place on a hill outside of Jerusalem.*

The Idea of Sacrament

Throughout this work we will use the word *sacrament* so often that the alert reader will guess that the word has a privileged place in the vocabulary of Catholicism. That guess would be right on target. Since we have already spoken about sacraments in passing with respect to the Eucharist we might best spend a few pages on the idea of sacrament and how the term is used in the Catholic theological tradition.

A sacrament, at bottom, is a sign. In the early Church the word was used in a wide sense to indicate anything that manifested the divine to humans. In that general sense the early theological writers described the Scriptures, religious rituals, Church teachings, and so on as sacraments (in Greek: *mysteries*). In that sense the sacrament is a visible reality (i.e. one that can be perceived in some fashion) which points to or shows forth something hidden, i.e. about God. In the long history of doctrinal reflection the idea was further specified so that by the Middle Ages it became usual to speak of seven sacraments in the Church. They are: baptism, confirmation, penance, holy Eucharist, matrimony, holy orders, and the anointing of the sick (once called extreme unction or the last anointing).

At this juncture we will use the term *sacrament* in the older and broader sense of the term. In that tradition we can affirm an ancient teaching of the Church that the great sign (*magnum sacramentum*) of God is Jesus himself. He is the outward and visible manifestation of God's concern for us. To grasp that concept we might recall a famous passage from the Epistle to the Hebrews:

---

*James Mackey, *Jesus: The Man and the Myth* (Ramsey: Paulist, 1979), p. 154.

In many and various ways God spoke of old to our fathers through
the prophets; but in these last days he has spoken to us by a Son
whom he appointed the heir of all things, through whom he also
created the world. He reflects the glory of God and bears the very
stamp of his nature, upholding the universe by his word of power
(Heb 1:1–3).

God communicated himself to the people of Israel through the patriarchs and the prophets but in Jesus God's presence is made visible
and tactile in a moment of real history. Jesus lived in the arena of human
affairs at a precise moment as a child born under the Jewish law and
born to a real woman (cf. Gal 4:4). Jesus was the concrete realization
of God's presence in the world. To encounter Jesus was to encounter
what God was like. He was the *incarnate* presence of God (incarnate
= in the flesh).

Thus, as a consequence of the above fact, it is quite appropriate to
call Jesus the sacrament of God. To pursue the point one step further:
if we think of the community of those who affirm Jesus as the Christ
not simply as an organization but as a community that bears witness to
Christ in time and space then we can also say, as did the early Church,
that the Church is also a sign/sacrament of Christ's continuing presence
in the world. In that sense the Church manifests Christ.

The Church, in turn, makes the reality of Christ present and specific by its use of sign/sacraments, the preeminent of which is the Eucharist. It is by understanding this dynamic link between Christ/Church
and Church/sign that we see that the sacrament is not some magical gesture but a communicated sign manifesting that the reality of the incarnate Christ still operates in the world. A sacrament is not a talisman; it
is a making concrete in time and space God's concern for the world and
its inhabitants. It does this through the quintessentially human act of the
visible gesture. Christ is a visible sign of God's love in the world, the
Church is a sign of the continuation of that presence, and the sacramental life of the Church makes that reality contact individuals and
communities. With specific reference to the Eucharist it is when we are
sharers in unity at the altar table that the clearest sign/sacrament of
God's love in Christ becomes palpably real.

There is an important corollary to be made at this point. It is this:
the Catholic religion is not an abstract set of beliefs or dogmas even

though it surely has beliefs and it does set out doctrines. Nor is the Catholic Church a "philosophy of life" nor an ethical system even though one can tease out a system of ethics and a set of philosophical guidelines from the Catholic tradition. The Catholic Church, first and foremost, is a visible witnessing community to the reality and perennial value of the life and meaning of Jesus the Christ. Its witness and life is to make visible the interest of God in us. It has a profound conviction that its office and *raison d'être* is to mediate God's presence in Christ to individuals and societies.

This desire to "make visible" also explains something about the context of the liturgy which we are observing in our hypothetical parish church. It is normally celebrated in the church building—a building which has its own architectural logic and its own peculiar form of decoration. The celebrant of the liturgy employs a stylized set of gestures (standing, bowing, bending the knee, etc.) while utilizing a whole series of vessels, books, vestments, and so on. The range of that stylized ceremonial may go from the extremely elaborate (think of a solemn liturgy in the Vatican with the Pope as celebrant) to the austere and simple worship conducted in a mission chapel. Whether complex or simple, the fact of ceremonial is a constant.

This ceremonial activity is not some form of mummery. Ceremony is a deeply human impulse which can be seen in our own home for festive meals. We put out the "best" dishes, real napkins, decorate the table with flowers, and arrange the seating of guests. We do not accept such gestures as "empty ritualism" or "mere show." As we have already noted, there is a very basic human impulse to formalize a meal setting. In the case of Catholic worship, the impulse toward ceremony and ritual is an aspect of Catholic incarnational theology.

Nobody would deny that ceremonial can be either extravagant or tasteless (or both) but that does not negate the basic idea in Catholic theology that visible gestures and manifestations are part of that deep religious impulse which accepts the sign value of created things. It is natural for a religion that preaches the idea of an *incarnate* God to desire to manifest that root conviction in as generous a way as possible. At its very best the formal celebration of the Eucharist declares in its very act of worship: this act is different, and the difference is intimately connected to beauty, ultimacy, solemnity, and religious meaning as we find those qualities in the very texture of created reality.

Eucharist and Tradition

If, to borrow the language of the schoolmen, we observe the accidents (as opposed to the substance) of the liturgy—the decorations in the church, the vestments, the appurtenances on the altar, etc.—it is not hard to see that our celebration does not take place in the same way as other acts of ordinary life do. Indeed, even in the most informal liturgies, much of the paraphernalia of the liturgy proclaims rather clearly that we are doing something quite out of the ordinary. To make the point more strongly: the kinds of things we do at the Sunday liturgy would appear quite out of place (even silly) were we to do them, say, in the main concourse of a shopping mall.

We can begin with something as simple as the dress of the celebrant—the long white gown (the alb) over which is worn either a broad stole or a more capacious outer garment called a chasuble. Such garments harken back to Roman times and may be seen in Christian art from the earliest centuries. The garments, in short, reflect not the contemporary world, but the ancient one. This is not the place to meditate on the history of vestments, but one point needs to be made with emphasis: the liturgy is not simply a "now" event; it reflects an historical memory and a feel for tradition.

The echoes of that tradition in the liturgy are complex and multilayered. Some elements of the liturgy reflect the deepest and oldest symbolic impulses of human religious consciousness which are given a particular Christian interpretation. The symbolic use of food, wine, water, light, and so on have analogues in many, if not most, religious traditions. They are quasi-universal in their meaning but given specific Christian interpretations in the context in which they are employed. As a noted historian of religion notes: "History adds new meanings, but they do not destroy the structure of the symbol."* Sacred meals have been with us from the beginning but this particular sacred meal has a specific and focused meaning.

Other gestures/symbols entered the liturgy at one specific moment in history with a very specific meaning, but over the centuries the meaning got lost so that now the gesture/symbol has a somewhat limited significance. Thus, for example, the genuflection (i.e. the reverential gesture of going down on one knee) once signified the fealty of a vassal

---

*Mircea Eliade, *The Sacred and the Profane* (New York: Harper Torchbook, 1961), p. 137.

to a lord in feudal times; it signified both a recognition of superiority and a pledge of fidelity. Today it is merely a stylized gesture of honor to God.

About these historical accretions to worship two things must be said. First, such gestures/symbols, when they can be meaningfully incorporated into the liturgy, emphasize the Church as a mind-ful community with a history and a tradition and, as such, link us, however tenuously, with some sense of the Church as living in time and space. Second, we need to keep old traditions in some kind of perspective. There is always the temptation to conserve for the sake of conservation: "This is the way we have always done it." Such temptations reduce tradition to mummification. Whatever is retained without meaning can always turn an act of worship into an act of magic, i.e. the sheer and plain manipulation of gestures. The Eucharist, while a formalized act of worship, is also a form of expression and reflective of belief. It is not—or, at least, it should not be—a mere stylized performance devoid of meaning.

The Catholic Church is not indifferent to the danger of being reduced to a museum of old symbols/gestures. When the late Pope John XXIII called for an *aggiornamento* (the Italian word means roughly an "updating") of the liturgy and the Church's practices, he was not calling for an abolition of tradition but only a clearing away of those accretions picked up in the course of time which obscured the message of the Gospel and its meaning. The liturgy of today, for example, is less hieratic, solemn, and ritualized than it was a generation ago, but the essential contours of the liturgy—the proclamation of the word of God, the celebration of the Eucharist—are much clearer. That, one would have to agree, is the heart of the matter.

There is another reason why a reasonable sense of the continuity of tradition should be maintained. The Eucharist should not be reduced to a celebration only of the here and now. To link the liturgy only to the concerns of the here and now is to risk irrelevancy in very short order. A colleague of mine, Professor Richard Rubenstein, once told me a story that forcefully illustrates the point. In the last century certain liberal German Jews, to show their antagonism to Zionism, began to substitute the traditional Passover prayer "Next year in Jerusalem" with a new prayer, one designed to show that they were assimilated into German culture: "Next year in Berlin." Only from the vantage point of history do we recognize how ghastly that change now seems to us.

A respect for tradition in our liturgical celebrations is an affirmation of our catholicity, a guard against trendiness, and a continuing challenge to our sensibilities. In the latter case we must allow for diversity and pluralism. It might seem odd or even distasteful to introduce the use of drums and accompanying dance to our liturgical celebrations; it would hardly seem odd for Amerindians to do so or for black Africans. In fact, in the Coptic liturgy of Ethiopia such usages are very old indeed. For that reason there must be a healthy balance between what is handed down ("tradition") and what must be newly employed. In this matter—as in so many—the old wisdom rings true: "In essentials, unity; in accidentals, liberty; in all things, charity."

The Eucharist and Daily Life

How does the celebration of the Eucharist relate to our ordinary life? At one level that is easy to answer. We "go to church" on Sunday to affirm something about the way we relate to the world. Our going to church (assuming it is not a matter of compulsion or sheer routine) says, by that gesture, that we recognize in our life something beyond the ordinary daily round of working, learning, loving, playing, and so on. We set aside—or step aside—for a time to do something out of the ordinary which says—to us, to our community, to our family—that we acknowledge a relationship with God in Christ.

That much is observable and clear. Yet we can pursue the meaning of that weekly gesture a bit further and a bit more personally. We can ask: What does this act mean not only to me as I understand it but as the Catholic tradition also understands it? If we begin to reflect on what the Church understands by worship we may find beliefs that are a bit more detailed than we ourselves are accustomed to express, but we can understand those beliefs as something toward which we might aspire.

First, the celebration of the weekly Eucharist is a collective gesture by which a gathered community expresses its faith in the risen Lord. The Eucharist is not merely a eulogy for a past historical figure but a re-enactment and a re-creation of the saving mysteries of the life, death, and resurrection of the Jesus whom we call Lord and Christ. We celebrate those mysteries *now* as a fulfillment of Christ's pledge that he is with us "until the end of time." In that sense the very celebration of the Eucharist is a profound social act of faith that Jesus is still present and active in the world.

Second, the Eucharist is a sign of the unity that exists among Christians. It is a visible bond of those who are reconciled to each other and to God (hence the confession of sin at the beginning of the liturgy and the gesture of peace before the reception of Communion). This particular union of a congregation has been often called by the ancient writers a microcosm of the unity of the great Church—*ecclesiola in ecclesia*. This basic unity in the Eucharist has been beautifully and poetically described in the *Didache,* one of the earliest non-biblical texts we possess from the ancient Church:

> As this broken bread was scattered over the hills and then, when gathered, became one mass, so may the Church be gathered from the ends of the earth unto thy kingdom. For thine is the glory and the power through Jesus Christ forevermore.

The prayer of the *Didache* does not see unity as already existing but something to come in the future. The Eucharist not only re-presents Christ to us now but points to the future when peace and reconciliation will be complete in Christ. As Paul said to the church at Corinth: we proclaim the death of Christ *until he comes* again. We all know from experience that our bonds of unity, even in the Eucharist, are as fragile as human ones can be. Everyone, alas, knows from experience that even members of the Church can be at odds or even in bitter and unseemly conflict. Thus, in the Eucharist we live a life of expectancy—we hope for the future in Christ.

If we regard the celebration of the Eucharist as a formal statement of our hopes and aspirations as Christian believers, it follows that there should be some correlation between our ordinary behavior and that which we formally profess; otherwise we are guilty of mere formalism and/or hypocrisy. It would be a travesty of Christ's message—and one often hears this charge made of believers—if ordinary lives were in direct conflict with what is formally professed in the liturgy.

We should not see in this issue only privatistic or moralistic lessons; it is not merely a question of being "free" from serious sin although that is obviously desirable. We need to learn how to spin out the full implications of what the liturgy proposes. When the fathers of the Second Vatican Council said that the sacramental life of the Church, and especially the Eucharist, "communicates and nourishes that charity which is the soul of the entire apostolate,"* they surely were insisting that we do something beyond merely leading a morally acceptable life. The Eucharist is connected with the entire apostolate of the Church.

The liturgy serves as the center and driving force for the life of the committed Christian. To live in the world as a Christian demands some link to the reality of Christ. That reality is best expressed in the proclamation of the word and the celebration of the body and blood of Christ. The liturgy, then, is a moment toward which we move and from which we again go to live and act in the world of ordinary life.

An authentic participation in the liturgy should also nourish in us a deeper sense of the *catholicity* (i.e. the universality) of the Church. At Mass we are in communion with each member of the community, with other communities in our area, and, finally, with all those communities which look to Peter's successor in Rome. That is the meaning behind the mentioning by name of both the local bishop and the current Pope in the liturgy. Some parishes are even attempting to twin themselves with a poorer parish in some other part of the world in order to share both the faith and material resources. Such a practice gives a deeper sense of catholicity and also acts as a practical and tangible means of "building up the body of Christ."

Points for Discussion

(a) In what sense, and under what circumstances, do I experience the liturgy as a *community* experience?

(b) Under what circumstances, and in what sense, do I experience the real presence of Christ in the liturgy?

(c) What strategies would be useful to make a connection with the celebration of the liturgy and one's ordinary workaday life?

(d) What most stands in the way of experiencing the liturgy as a living religious experience? Have liturgical modifications been helpful (do we need more? less?) in making the liturgy live?

(e) It is often alleged that the reformed liturgy has removed the sense of "mystery" from the liturgy. Is that a fair judgment? If so, what would be some possible remedies for that sense of lack?

Decree on the Apostolate of the Laity I.3 in *Documents*, p. 492.

Chapter IV

Christian Community Observed

It is worthwhile to take a look around a typical North American parish congregation some Sunday. I did just that last week and noted the following: the congregation was, by and large, white and middle class with a sprinkling of blacks, Asiatics (including the celebrant who is from the Philippines), and an Indian family complete with the mother in a sari. There were all age groups and few clear indicators of class distinction: very few people were flamboyantly rich or strikingly poor looking.

I ask myself: How did all these people end up in this particular Church which we call the Catholic Church?

Some, obviously, are here because they are born Catholics and they are doing what their families have done for untold generations. Others are here—I know a few of them—because for one reason or another they converted and became Catholics. A few, like the bored and sulky teenager in front of me, are here because either their family or custom made them be here. One can only guess at the motives which bring people to worship on Sunday; the motives, one suspects, range from habit or compulsion to a sense of duty or the feeling of real need.

A Catholic congregation, like any human gathering, is, on close inspection, a very complex reality. The complexity becomes all the more clear when we get away from a rather homogeneous group like an American parish (or an African or Irish one, for that matter) and attend, say, a ceremony at St. Peter's in the Vatican. Apart from the curious tourist, we see a gabble of races, a symphony of foreign tongues, colorfully clad members of various religious orders, members of the Vatican curia, dignitaries ranging from black African cardinals to bearded patriarchs of the Oriental Church. On a great feastday like Christmas or Easter the Pope may greet visitors in forty or fifty languages.

The Catholic community is varied not only in actual diversity of race, nationality, and color. It is varied in the history it brings to its Catholicism. Roman Catholics from some parts of Africa or the Far East may trace their ancestry in the faith back only a generation or two. Other cultures and lands have been Catholic for nearly two millennia.

57

I have often wondered myself for how many generations my Lithuanian and Irish ancestors have been attending Mass. The point is this: the sense of Catholic community extends not only to the actualities of today but back in history as well.

What do all these people, those in history, as well as our contemporaries, have in common?

The obvious answer is that they all identify themselves as Catholics no matter what their nationality, social class, race, or sex. One great difficulty is that we dare not generalize about what people think or believe. At times we merely have a social profile of what a Catholic *ought* to be like. We say that Mister X is a good Catholic because of his name (Ryan), his education (Fordham), his affiliations (Knights of Columbus), his family size (six kids), and his job (police lieutenant in New York City). Such a social profile tells us a good deal and very little. Using those social criteria we might miss a person who rarely attends church, has no visible social affiliations, yet feels some deep, if not clearly articulated, bond to the Church. What is one to make of a philosopher like the late George Santayana or the British novelist Graham Greene, people who describe themselves as "Catholic atheists"?

We might get at the question of Catholic identity by an approach which is less socially oriented and more directed to theological categories. Before we begin to do that there are two preliminary observations which need to be made.

(a) The new Code of Canon Law gives us a succinct definition of who is a member of the Catholic community: "Christ's faithful are those who, since they are incorporated into Christ through baptism, are constituted the people of God."*

In the definition of the Code, then, it is the rite of baptism which is decisive for defining who is, and who is not, a Catholic. It should be noted, however, that this definition is a legal or judicial one and, as such, should be understood in that restrictive sense. Napoleon Bonaparte, for example, was a baptized Catholic and would be treated as such as far as the Code is concerned; Napoleon, however (or Fidel Castro, to give a more contemporary example), is hardly an exemplar of what the Church thinks a Catholic ought to be.

---

*Canon 204–#1.

Nonetheless, we can insist, with the Code of Canon Law, that the sacrament of baptism is decisive in determining membership in the Catholic community. Hence, our second general observation:

(b) Baptism is the sign-sacrament by which a person "puts on Christ." By the symbolic cleansing with water, warranted by numerous passages in the New Testament, people pass from the old life of sin and bondage into the new life of grace. St. Paul sees baptism as a kind of death/rebirth. Just as Jesus died, was buried, and rose again, so the Christian goes into the waters and undergoes a kind of symbolic resurrection by emerging as a new person cleansed in Christ. It is because of the deep symbolism of baptism's connection with the saving mysteries of Christ that the Church from the very beginnings of its history linked the sacrament of baptism with the celebration of Easter. People who attend the vigil services on the eve of Easter cannot but be impressed by the numerous allusions to baptism (including the blessing of water) and the actual baptism of new converts.

When Paul mentioned baptism he clearly had adult baptism in mind. The Church, from its earliest days, also baptized infants long before they could freely choose to be Christians. It is hoped that the infant, upon reaching a more mature age, will make a fundamental option for the faith, and, in that act, confirm by an act of the will what has been done for him/her through the agency of the Church and the wishes of his or her family. This is not a frivolous hope since the Church has always believed that baptism is an effective sign of God's favor to the person who receives it. For the baptized person who consents in faith there flows a number of real consequences: forgiveness of sin, a new life in God, incorporation into the life of the Church, and participation in the new covenant promised by Jesus.

Two Metaphors of Community

Body of Christ: Baptism, then, is the sign-sacrament of our entrance in the worshiping community. We can now make this further inquiry: How are we to understand that body or community of baptized believers who attempt to follow Christ? Is it to be understood as a kind of voluntary club or as something more intimate like a family or as a highly structured organization like a legal corporation? One way to an-

swer that question is to ask about the description(s) that the Church itself provides in order to explain itself.

When we look into the pages of the New Testament we note rather
quickly that there are a number of metaphors employed to describe the
body of followers of Christ. In a wonderfully rich section of the Second
Vatican Council's *Dogmatic Constitution on the Church* (I.6) there is
a long listing of some of the more prominent biblical images of the
Church: the sheepfold, the flock of God, the land to be cultivated, the
edifice of God, a living temple, a holy city, the heavenly Jerusalem, a
mother, a spouse, and, most significantly, a body; or, to be more precise, the body of Christ.

It is that latter metaphor—the body of Christ—that we wish to begin with. Note this seminal passage from St. Paul in the New Testament:

> For just as the body is one and has many members, and all the mem-
> bers of the body, though many, are one, so it is with Christ. For by
> one spirit we were all baptized into one body—Jews or Greeks,
> slaves or free—and all were made to drink of the one spirit
> (1 Cor 12:12–13).

First, and foremost, then, the church is to be thought of—like a
body—as a living organic reality. The deepest meaning of being in the
Church, setting aside sociological considerations, is that sense of being
bound together in a deep way with other believers in Christ. This organic unity also implies, as the above passage makes abundantly clear,
that there is a homogeneity in that unity. In that sense, no single member is "better" or "more exalted" or of more worth. Paul says that
Jews/Greeks and males/females (the disjunctions mean—as is clear—
everyone) all participate in that same spirit. What Paul envisions is a
body with the head being Christ; we are the members of that body, taking our sustenance and sensing our unity as coming from the "head-
ship" of Christ.

In the same epistle Paul draws a lesson from this sense of organic
unity: "That there may be no discord in that body, but that the members
may have the same care for one another. If one member suffers, all
suffer together; if one member is honored, all rejoice together" (1 Cor
12:25–26). Not to put too fine a point on it: this organic community in
Christ is a community of responsibility, or, better, co-responsibility.

It is that imperative of co-responsibility which sheds a lot of light on the idea of the Church as *catholic;* catholicity is our theme and we shall return to it time and again in these pages. Catholic means universal and at least one sense of that term implies that the authentic Catholic cultivates a sense of inter-connectedness with Christ as head and with those who make up our local believing community and the universal *ecclesia* which can be thought of as the aggregation of all the local communities of faith bound together under Christ. Translating that notion into specifics means simply that a Catholic in this wealthy society of the West cannot be indifferent to the material sufferings of a Catholic in Central America or the spiritual sufferings of a Catholic in the Ukraine. To be indifferent to the body of the Church fails the organic unity of the Church, the body of Christ, and diminishes, simultaneously, the catholicity of the Church.

We do not accept the notion that this organic reality is a single one. The Catholic Church has never accepted the idea of being a perfectionist group made up only of the saintly and those already perfected in Christ. We remember the parable of the field which has both wheat and weeds in it. One sign of our sinfulness as a body is our willingness, at the beginning of each liturgical assembly, to confess our sins as a body and to ask again—yet again—for forgiveness. That simple rite—repeated every day in Catholic worship—symbolizes forcefully the Catholic conviction that only at the end of history will all sinfulness and imperfection, characteristic of life on earth, be healed and reconciled.

The Pilgrim Church: One other metaphor, highlighted in the documents of the Second Vatican Council, helps us to grasp more fully the historical and organic character of the Church as a community; it is the metaphor of the pilgrimage.

In these days of mass tourism ("Join our ten day tour of Rome and the Holy Land") in which jet lag is the major inconvenience, it is very difficult to recapture the sense of pilgrimage as it was experienced by earlier generations of Christians who went on foot to the great pilgrimage sites of Europe and the Holy Land. Pilgrimage was such a crucial part of the religious experience of the Middle Ages that it added a whole vocabulary, both in literature and art, to the traditional understanding of pilgrimage as a religious act. Pilgrimage, as many scholars have demonstrated over the years, contributed to the development of commerce, warfare, art, literature, social change, and religious understanding. The greatest works of medieval literature—one need only cite

Dante and Chaucer—are rooted in the language of pilgrimage. When Dante finished his great imaginative journey through hell, purgatory, and the spheres of heaven, he was given a momentary glance at the majesty of God who was at the very center of the universe as a source of light and love. In the moment of that vision Dante reached for one of the most common metaphors of his time to describe his emotions:

> And like a pilgrim who is refreshed in the church of his vow
> As he looks about and hopes to tell of it again
> So, moving my eyes up through the living light,
> Looked, now up, now down, and then around again
>   (*Paradiso* xxxi: 43–48).

The very nature of a pilgrimage is defined by the intention of a pilgrim to move toward a goal. The pilgrim is not a vagrant wanderer. Pilgrimage is arduous, done from a spiritual motive, and available to anyone who wishes to go on a journey. It is in that sense that pilgrimage as a metaphor for being in the Church must be understood. The Church is a company (*cum pane*—bread sharers) of people, as variegated as Chaucer's pilgrims, who move through time and space, toward a goal. The journey has its own difficulties, made easier by mutual concern and mutual help, but its purpose is clear. The key to thinking about pilgrimage, however, is that it is a process of going; the goal has not been reached—it is only attainable.

Because the pilgrim Church is "not yet there," it has not attained its purpose; it has not yet fulfilled its promise; it is *in via*. That is a crucial point to remember. Catholicism is not a perfectionist sect which insists that its members are perfect or the elect, free from, and antagonistic toward, the world around it. The Church sees itself, rather, as a community of people, fragile but open in faith, insecure in virtue, who look for inspiration to Jesus Christ who is, simultaneously, the yardstick to measure failure, the source of its continuing faith, and the end (*telos*) of its journey. Pilgrimage, almost by definition, signifies, not a goal attained, but a yearning for that attainment.

There is an important lesson to be drawn from this metaphor of pilgrimage. It is this: we should expect no more of the Church as a communal reality of pilgrims than we expect of ourselves. It is always painful to hear of this or that person who is bitterly alienated from the Church because of the behavior of a particular pilgrim (the venal priest, the uncaring neighbor, the harsh functionary), but one must realize that such behavior is understandable (but not necessarily excusable) when we honestly confront the fact that we also are capable of greed, harshness, and indifference. The Church as a company of pilgrims is "not yet there" and, as a consequence, reflects (and, to a degree, magnifies) all of the meanness and frailty of the imperfect humans that we are. That is why I like to go back to the prologue of Chaucer's *Canterbury Tales*. It is such a humane understanding of the Church as a pilgrimage. We find the odious pardoner, the rascally friar, the over-refined prioress, as well as the extremely likeable wife of Bath, the noble knight, the zealous student, and, of course, the Christ-like parson. They are all headed to a destination and all, to a greater and lesser degree, motivated by a common faith.

Structures

The Church, then, following our two metaphors of body and pilgrimage, can be thought of as an organic community on a voyage toward a goal. In both images we have a picture of large numbers of people. How, in real terms, are these people related and connected to each other? What visible social bonds distinguish them from other communities including other religious ones? What structures make this community different from another one?

Those questions can be answered in a number of different ways. We could say that all Christians who live in unity with the bishop of Rome (i.e. the Pope) or who live in conformity to a certain set of doctrinal truths or who worship in a peculiar way (the word *orthodoxy* means "correct worship") define the structures in a certain manner. Those are all issues which we will take up in due course. For the moment we wish to underscore two other ways in which we discover that larger unity which we call Catholicism.

In the first place we can think of our Catholic community as existing in spatial terms; in other words: Catholic reality is found *in place*. Let us, for a moment, again consider our hypothetical parish. It is—if it is typical—a discrete geographical slice of a city or town with a pastor assigned to oversee its religious life. A number of parishes may make up a diocese with a bishop overseeing that geographical reality; in turn, several dioceses may make up an archdiocese and the sum total of them (allowing for exceptions regarding different rites and/or missionary arrangements) making up the "Church as a whole." It is possible, in short, to think of the Church as a world-wide observable phenomenon divided into manageable spatial units based, largely, on the peculiarities of geography.

Is that a useful way of thinking about the Church? It is certainly a traditional way of thinking about it as a visible reality, but some critics think that undue emphasis on the Church as a visible organization extended out in space leads too many to think of the Church as a megacorporation: the Church as a spiritual multinational. I think that this is a valid criticism if we think of the Church from "top to bottom," i.e. the Pope giving orders to the dioceses while the dioceses give orders to the parishes who, in turn, from the pulpit, instruct the layperson in the pew. There has been a good deal of that kind of thinking about the Church, and the Church, since the Second Vatican Council, has resisted such formulations. It makes the Church seem too rigid, too monolithic, and too heartless.

But there is another approach that we can take which integrates the notion of the Church as a geographical reality while still being faithful to the metaphors of organic unity and pilgrimage which we have discussed above. We can think small and simply reflect on the parish itself.

A simple look around a typical parish can help us see the point. The parish as an organized reality existing within spatial parameters is, in reality, a kind of umbrella for all kinds of activities that feed the varied needs of the parishioners (and others who live in the parish boundaries) in their pilgrimage. A look at a typical parish bulletin will reveal everything from social groups, study circles, and clubs for children to various outreach organizations concerned with issues of justice and charity. There are also movements which aid the larger concerns of the diocese and those of the universal Church. Parishioners are reminded regularly of not only local needs but also those of the larger world. The parish is (or, better, should be) a local reality which has ties to larger ones. What the parish is, finally, is a very human manifestation to form social bonds which express a common core of symbols and aspirations.

The parish is a canonical structure: a reality which exists because it is prescribed in the canon law of the Church. It is not the only one by any means. Besides the various canonical structures in the Church (like religious orders) there is a bewildering variety of voluntary organizations which grow up parallel to regular Church structures. Catholics, like everyone else, bind themselves together for an infinite variety of reasons. They may join together as farmers, workers, intellectuals, or what not. They may form associations for more focused social needs or spiritual enrichment or certain forms of organized charity. The reason for this wide variety of voluntary organizations is that the Church accepts the idea that there are a wide range of religious sensibilities which must be tended and fed in the Church. When one looks beyond the variety, one sees that there are (or should be) certain constants of belief and practice with a wide latitude of expressions and usages. The Catholic Peace Fellowship is not the same as Catholics United for the Faith which is not the same as the St. Vincent de Paul Society which is not the same as the League of the Sacred Heart. What one does hope is that what divides them into groups is not as important as what makes them all call themselves "Catholic."

The point to be underscored is this: while it is possible to think of a kind of overarching structure to Catholic life (summed up in the parish/diocese/papal office structure) there are, in reality, all kinds of organizations, movements, communities, and so on which work within (or at the edges of) such a structure. What all of these experiments have in common is a basic affirmation of the faith handed down by the Church. There is nothing absolute or sacrosanct about parish life (the recent explosion of "base communities"—small groups of people who gather for Scripture study and worship—is a reaction against one kind of parish life) but, whatever its deficiencies, it still can be flexible enough for other kinds of community to take place.

Catholicism puts a very strong emphasis on community, on the social nature of religion. From that easily observable fact we can deduce a goodly number of things about the Catholic experience. It may be useful at this point to list some of the more salient deductions we can make.

First, the Catholic emphasis on community stands in rather sharp contrast to certain kinds of Protestant fundamentalism with its equally strong emphasis on individuality. When the now ubiquitous television preachers call for a "personal commitment" from the audience and a public repudiation of sin, they are asking for nothing with which a Catholic could quarrel. All of us need to express our unworthiness and all of us need to commit ourselves to Christ in faith. Catholics would only note that these television preachers lack a very real nuance. Catholics do not see conversion to God in Christ as a rigidly vertical affair which concerns only the individual and God. Surely we must take personal responsibility for our life and make a personal commitment in faith. Catholics would then hasten to add that God calls us not to individual conversion alone but to be members of a witnessing community which is to be a sign of Christ's presence in the world. Christian conversion has, then, both a personal and a social aspect to it. We are converted (i.e. turned toward) to Christ in community. We are called to be children of God and to membership in the people of God.

Second, Catholicism does not see itself as a loose federation of individual communities tied together only by some administrative bonds. The authentic sense of Catholic community, rooted in the metaphors of body and pilgrimage, indicates an organic unity. Thus, the Catholic Church is enhanced and/or diminished to the degree that this or that particular Catholic community realizes its intimate connection with the whole Church. Local communities, as an essential part of being called Catholic, need to nourish a sense of global community. In the concrete, that means that a Catholic in this or that particular locale must be concerned with the concerns of the Pope just as much as the Pope must serve the needs of the local community. Similarly, we aid the missions or the less fortunate parts of the Church not out of a niggardly sense of charity but because that is what it means to be a Catholic. We need the heroic witness of the impoverished world just as much as they need (or, better, have a right to) our excess and our riches. To be indifferent to the needs of the whole Church is a diminishment of the virtue of catholicity.

Third, this sense of organic community—and we can never emphasize this fact too often—embraces not just those communicants who live in the here and now. Because the Catholic Church sees itself as rooted in the New Testament's witness it is necessary for the Church to constantly look back to test its current practice by the yardstick of the inherited tradition of the Church. If the Church is anything, it is a community of memory. This remembering takes many and diverse forms. A religious order may have to look back to see if it is faithful to the fundamental insights of its founder. The Church as a whole constantly asks if this or that particular practice faithfully reflects the tradition from whence this or that practice comes. Things like liturgical renewal, after all, are nothing more than attempts to be faithful to its past.

In re-searching our past we place ourselves in continuity with those who have gone before us in the faith. In that sense we can get a better understanding about the Church's concern with its past saints, heroes, founders, and so on. Those people witness to the attempt at fidelity in the past and from them we can learn about the present. The Church holds on to the *nova et vetera*—the new things and the old which are part of the continuing witness of the Church.

We not only look to the past as a community but also to the future. In that sense, the Church is never fully Catholic; it strives for catholicity and fullness which will come, as the Scriptures say, only in the fullness of God's good time. This sentiment of striving toward future perfection is evocatively expressed in a wonderful passage from the Second Vatican Council:

> Even now on this earth the Church is marked with a genuine but imperfect holiness. However, until there is a new heaven and a new earth (cf. 2 Peter 3:13), the pilgrim Church in her sacraments and institutions, which pertain to the present time, takes on the appearance of this passing world. She herself dwells among creatures who groan and travail in pain until now and await the revelation of the Son of God (cf. Rom 8:19–22).*

Fourth, the time-bound community which is the Church, as the above citation makes abundantly clear, is on the way but is an imperfect vessel. The consequences of that fact are enormous but often imperfectly understood or glossed over. However much we may be nourished by thinking of the Church in the great theological and biblical metaphors we have enunciated, it remains a fact that the reality of the Church is the reality of this really existing historical reality which we call the Church. We cannot reduce the Church to some idealized platonic idea free from the grittiness of historical reality. This parish, that diocese, or yonder papacy *is* the Church. The Church *in via* is no better or worse than those who make it up. We can look around a particular community at worship and see the heroically virtuous (that family in the next pew that lovingly cares for an afflicted child) as well as the nominal pew warmer who is there to keep up appearances or to insure the "Catholic trade" for his shop or business. That congregation is the Church in microcosm.

From the above observations we can understand that in the Church there will always be imperfection, sin, scandal, and shocking indifference. That is not a situation that one glories in; it is, however, a fact

*Dogmatic Constitution on the Church VII.48, in Documents, p. 79.

which needs to be stated. People are often scandalized by the unworthiness of Church members (and rightly so). The credibility of the Church, and its efficacy, have often been harmed by such behavior. At times it has been of such a magnitude as to take on a deeply symbolic meaning for large numbers of people outside the Church. Catholics need face up to the fact and, in facing it, do reparation for it. But if we think again of our organic metaphors we can say—and this is not a pious evasion nor an exaggeration—that the manifest weaknesses of the Church and its members can be viewed as a kind of anti-sacrament which reflects our imperfection and our groping toward the "not yet" of the future. The blemishes of the Church, some very deep indeed, remind us with stunning force of our need for grace, our need for mutual concern, support, and compassion, and our need for trust in the goodness of God. The weakness of the Church is, paradoxically, a guarantee of the continuing relevance of faith and trust.

The Catholic community, to repeat, is in the process of being built. The call of Christ (our *vocation*) is not designed only for working out "my" salvation understood in an individualistic manner; we are called upon—we have a vocation for—the building up of the body of Christ which is the Church. That is not merely an option for a Christian; it is an obligation so derived from the call of Christ so that Christ should "rule in your hearts, to which you were called in the one body" (Col 3:15).

That sense of social conversion helps us to get a better understanding of the notion of "sin" since sin is the other side of the coin from conversion. When we turn to God (convert) we turn away from (avert) those things which keep God in abeyance. Sin involves a choice against God and not merely a breaking of rules, even if they are God's rules. Sin involves a turning away from God, a refusal of God's self-gift in Christ. The act of sin, for which we must take personal responsibility (since *I* choose or *I* acquiesce), is also a social act in the sense that our failure/alienation harms the organic reality of the Church and of human community. When we speak of sinful structures we are really talking about that passivity of all individuals in the face of institutional evil. Sin, as it spreads in the Church and in human society, can appear in a luridly conspicuous fashion (as it surely has in certain places and/or periods of the Church's life) or it may be a kind of creeping diminution of God's reality in a concrete circumstance. In either case, the making present of the reality of Christ is diminished. It is only when we fully understand that fact that it becomes possible to fully appreciate why the public confession of sin which prefaces each liturgy is not merely a *pro forma* exercise in humility even when we treat it as such.

The community of believers shows itself as a structured and living reality best when it is gathered for worship. That is the clearest sign of its visible reality. It is there that we ask forgiveness, refresh ourselves with the word of God, enter in Communion with Christ, and then go forth to our lives. In the workaday world the fruits of the Church are present when, as individuals or as communities, we represent what we profess in visible gestures and activities.

Where then is the Church?

It is in the parish at worship, at the table of a family eating together, in the doing of charity and justice, in witness to the love of Christ, in the acceptance and alleviation of suffering, in the work of reconciliation, in the silence of meditation, in the business of doing what ought to be done. It is, in short, everywhere that the face of Christ is made visible either by an individual or when two or three are gathered together in Christ's name.

Points for Discussion

(a) How would you profile your own parish as a Christian community?

(b) What concrete and specific suggestions would you make to give your own worshiping community a greater sense of unity and cohesiveness?

(c) What do you consider the greatest obstacles to a sense of catholicity in your own Christian life?

(d) Under what circumstances, and for what reasons, do you have a sense of being unified to the great Church tradition of Catholicism? How would you like to gain a better sense of that catholicity?

(e) Do you normally think of the Church as an "organization" or do you have a deeper sense of the Church as community? How can that latter sense of community be cultivated? How much personal responsibility can you accept to foster such a sense?

Chapter V

The *Roman* Catholic Church

In the previous chapter we described a number of terms which are useful when thinking about the Church as a community. The unsentimental reader might object that, while that chapter may contain many and rich theological observations about an idealized Church, the plain fact of the matter is that the Catholic community's most distinguishing characteristic is that it is the only organized Christian body in the world which gives allegiance to, and allows special prerogatives for, the bishop of Rome, known more familiarly as the Pope.

That point is unimpeachable and must be fairly discussed. The Roman Catholic Church does share a common liturgical tradition with the Orthodox and Anglican communions and a common faith with them and all Protestants who affirm Jesus as the Christ and the Scriptures as the word of God, but what all these Christian churches have in common is their rejection of the papal office as it is understood in the Roman Catholic Church as well as the claims that the Roman Catholic Church makes for the papacy. To understand Catholicism as a visible and organized Church, then, one must understand the papacy. *Ubi Petrus, ibi ecclesia* (''Where Peter is, there is the church'') is an old Roman Catholic rallying cry.

A close study of the papacy both as an historical institution and as a theological concept deepens our sense of Catholicism and provides us with a close view of the entangling webs of history, culture, belief, and reflection that are part and parcel of every religious tradition with an historical memory. The fact that the papacy evolved in tandem with what we call Western culture (the papacy was over a thousand years old when Columbus set foot on the shores of the New World) makes the tracing of this story an impossible task in a book of this modest size. While we would like to think of the office of the papacy only in terms of Peter's role in the New Testament Church, our historical imagination will allow us no simplification. In fact, we might note in passing that the place of Peter in the New Testament is far more complicated than either Catholic or Protestant theologians have allowed in the past.*

---

*One of the urgent tasks of ecumenical discussion is to understand the role of Peter in the

73

When we say the word "Pope" or "papacy" people do not generally think of Peter in the New Testament. Instead, they think of tiaras, the Vatican, "good Popes" (John XXIII) or "bad popes" (Alexander VI), flamboyant processions, art treasures, and, increasingly, worldwide tours of Popes meeting huge and generally adulatory crowds. This whole range of impressions derives from both the reading of history and the impact of satellite-fed television. It is too easy to get caught up with images, so we might want to keep them in the back of our minds (we probably cannot erase them anyway) while trying to understand the papacy in somewhat more manageable terms. We might try to frame our basic question(s) for this chapter in the following fashion:

Let us assume, for the sake of argument, that the office of the papacy derives from the ministry of Peter in the New Testament. How did the office of that simple apostle evolve, in time, to an office of such Cecil B. De Milleish proportions which we see on television today? What was the dynamic that got us from there to here? The issue, in a larger form, was acidly framed in the last century by Ernest Renan who quipped that Jesus preached the kingdom of God and we ended up with the Catholic Church.

The Papacy as Institution

The Catholic Church sees itself—as it says in the creed—as an *apostolic* Church, i.e. a community which looks back to the apostles of the New Testament community as its founders. It is from this fact of apostolicity that the role of the Pope in the Catholic Church must be understood. The teaching of the Second Vatican Council sets out this basic doctrine in detail. It can serve as a starting point for us:

> In order to establish this holy church of his everywhere in the world
> until the end of time, Christ entrusted to the college of the Twelve
> the task of teaching, ruling, and sanctifying. Among their number
> he chose Peter. After Peter's profession of faith, he decreed that on
> him he would build his Church; to Peter he promised the keys to
> the kingdom of heaven (cf. Mt 16:19 in comparison with Mt 18:18).

---

early Church and his relationship to what eventually came to be known as the papal office. The indispensable work on this topic is Raymond E. Brown *et al.*, *Peter in the New Testament* (New York: Paulist, 1973).

After Peter's profession of love, Christ entrusted all his sheep to him to be confirmed in faith (cf. Lk 22:32) and shepherded in perfect unity (cf. Jn 21:15–17). Meanwhile, Christ Jesus himself forever remains the chief cornerstone (cf. Eph. 2:20) and shepherd of souls.

It is through the faithful preaching of the Gospel by the apostles and their successors—the bishops with Peter's successor at their head—through their administration of the sacraments, and through their loving exercise of authority, that Jesus Christ wishes his people to increase under the influence of the Holy Spirit.*

History, of course, is not as tidy as a theological formulation like the one cited above. In the first centuries of the Church's life it became usual (and not without some good historical reasons) to think of the bishop (i.e. the "overseer") of the Church of Rome as a lineal successor to the apostle Peter. That ancestry, and the fact that Rome was the seat of the empire, gave prestige to the bishop of Rome. In subsequent centuries the bishop of Rome came to be looked upon—and often claimed to be—*the* head of the universal Church even though the claim was disputed in the Middle Ages by the patriarch of Constantinople and, of course, by the reformers in the sixteenth century.

Despite such denials from the world of Orthodoxy and the Reformation, Catholic theology argued that the office of the papacy was supreme in the spiritual realm because of Christ's express gift of the "keys" to Peter. For complex historical reasons the Popes in the medieval period began to restrict to themselves Church powers which were once much more widely dispersed in the Church: the right to canonize saints, to call councils, to name bishops, to regulate the liturgy, etc. This all happened during an historical epoch when the Popes reigned over lands—thought to be theirs by legitimate right—as a temporal monarch. It is for this reason that the Popes in the Middle Ages present to us such a complex and bewildering picture with religious, social, economic, and political features obscuring the essential theological character of the office. A supremely orthodox writer like Dante in *The Divine Comedy* saw no contradiction at all in pointing out a place in his imagined hell for a Pope who was then reigning while, later, in the same poem, he could have a character excoriate a king who laid violent hands

---

*The Decree on Ecumenism, I.2, in *Documents*, p. 344. That excerpt reproduces, in condensed form, standard Roman Catholic teaching about apostolicity and the role of bishops in the Church.

on that same evil Pope. For Dante there was an essential distinction to be made between the office of the Pope and the person who happened, historically, to hold it.

As we all know, one of the leading grievances of the sixteenth century reformers had to do with the pretensions, corruption, and power of the papacy. For Luther and his followers it was not a question of reforming the papacy; they wanted it abolished. For the reformers the Pope was the great whore of Babylon predicted by John in the Book of Revelation. The one thing that all the reformers had in common was the unassailable conviction that the Pope was the anti-Christ.

It was inevitable, given the reformers' fierce rejection of the papacy, that the Catholic Church, after the sixteenth century, should have emphasized the legitimacy of the papal office and used that defense as a kind of a polemical tool against the Protestants. Indeed, given the nature of violent and argumentative confrontations, it was also inevitable that the Catholic Church should seek ways of enhancing the office of the Pope. The culmination of this process came in 1869–70 when the First Vatican Council not only reaffirmed the primacy of the Pope as the visible head of the Church but formally defined—after a bitter and acrimonious debate—that the Pope was infallible when he taught on matters pertaining to faith and morals.

Given the momentous importance of that conciliar definition—and the controversies and confusions surrounding it subsequently—we should note what the Council did and did not do. In July 1870 the First Vatican Council solemnly affirmed that Peter had been chosen by Christ as head of the apostolic college and that the primacy of Peter resided, *in perpetuo,* in the Roman Pontiff, i.e. the Pope. The Council then went on to affirm, as a matter of revealed Christian truth, that the Pope, when he solemnly taught the entire Church on a matter of faith and morals in his capacity as supreme pastor of the Church, was infallible. This infallibility, the Council affirmed, derived from the personal office of the papacy and not from the power invested in his person by the entire Church.

What, specifically, does that teaching mean? What exactly is papal infallibility? We can begin with some exclusions. It does *not* mean that the Pope personally enjoys a greater morality or is spiritually superior to other members of the Church. History would reject any claim that the popes were impeccable. It does *not* mean that the Pope can serve as a conduit of new revelations. It does *not* mean that every utterance of the Pope, even on solemn occasions, is free from error or ambiguity. It does *not* mean that the Pope is immune from error in matters of faith or morals in his own personal thinking.

What papal infallibility does mean, in a positive sense, is this: When the Pope solemnly instructs the entire Church in his capacity as head of the Church on a matter pertaining to what the Church believes and/or how the Church views a particular moral issue, he will not speak erroneously and lead the Church away from the authentic sources of revelation. The gift of papal infallibility should be understood essentially as a negative one: the grace not to lead the Church into error. Papal infallibility does not mean that the Pope will say anything "new" or even particularly enlightening. It might be well to note here in passing that, using the strict criteria articulated at the First Vatican Council, the Popes of modern times have rarely used their prerogative. Apart from the definition of Mary's assumption in 1950 by the late Pope Pius XII, it is difficult to point to another example of infallible papal teaching in the modern period.

When the First Vatican Council defined the doctrine of papal infallibility it did not go on to relate that teaching on papal power to the teaching authority (often called the *magisterium*) of the entire Church. The Council, because of war in Europe, came to an abrupt and unceremonious end. The Second Vatican Council (1962–65) issued further reflections on the collegial nature of the episcopacy, on the voice of the laity, and on the need for the Church to listen and be instructed by "the signs of the times" with such emphasis that *practically speaking* the idea of the Pope speaking infallibly without wide consultation and a collegial consensus seems a rather unlikely happening in the future.

The Papacy: Some Reflections

The two traditional Catholic affirmations of papal primacy and papal infallibility are the two great teachings about the papal office. It might be useful to articulate some concrete observations of a less theoretical nature which will aid us in understanding the papacy in the life of the Catholic Church and in the larger Christian world.

In the first place, we must remember that the papal office (often referred to now by the more scriptural term as the *Petrine ministry*) as it exists today carries with it nearly two millennia of historical baggage. The entire complex of the Vatican which, for many, symbolizes the papacy is incredibly old. In the decade that Columbus sailed for the New World it was decided to rebuild St. Peter's Basilica in the Vatican. The old building was then a thousand years old!

If I insist on the point of the antiquity of the papacy, it is not for antiquarian reasons. There is another point. One must not confuse the historical baggage for what is essential. This is not a first step observation intended to junk the panoply and tradition of the Vatican (it has its own logic and beauty) but a plea to recognize its essentially peripheral nature when we ask the hard questions about how the Petrine ministry contributes to, and is essential for, the Catholic community.

Second, we must remember that the office of the papacy functions for Catholics as a visible sign of the Church's unity. No particular community (e.g. the Irish church or the Chilean church) is totally and fully autonomous. When we speak of the American church or the silent church or the church of the poor we must remember that what makes them all Catholic is not their Americanness or their poverty or their condition of oppression but their bond—however tenuous at times—with the center of unity which is invested in the papacy.

It should be obvious, however, that unity can often by a slight step get confused with uniformity. Partially as a result of the Protestant Reformation the modern Catholic Church put a great emphasis on a uniformity understood as compliance to Roman standards: there were Roman vestments, a Roman liturgy, a Roman theology, an attitude called "thinking with Rome." Such an emphasis on centralization gave the Church a strong sense of internal discipline that served the Church well in the post-Reformation period. The price of that discipline, however, was a certain rigidity and, not infrequently, a mindless conformity.

This is an age, given the revolution in communications, in which the world understands the plurality and integrity of diverse cultures. In the face of such a fact the great task of the contemporary Church is to account for cultural diversity and, simultaneously, to hold on to a sense of unity in that diversity. Religious experience is mediated through culture, and a singular culture (Roman or European or Western) may not suffice for the needs of all people in all places. We need a plurality of religious expression within the parameters of Catholic unity. That is easier to state as a theoretical principle than it is to carry out in practice. How, for example, does the Church in Africa or Asia stay Catholic without assuming all of the thought patterns and historical trapping of

Roman Christianity? Is it right, to use an oft cited example, to demand celibacy of an African cleric when the very heart of African social reality rests on the notion of the family and its extensions? Why celibacy when there is nothing in their cultural heritage which prepares for such a state of life? While celibacy may be an effective sign for the West, is it an effective sign for Africa? Is celibacy enforced in the African church merely because it is part of the uniform discipline of the Church? To all those questions one might find very different points of view. But it is one example of the kind of issue which tests the diversity/unity tension in the Church.

In the third place, while the papal function is traditionally described as "teaching, ruling, and sanctifying" the Church, we should also take note of its function as *servant* of the universal Church. That concept is particularly satisfying for this age. For a long time it has been common to think of the Pope as a completely autonomous and supremely competent monarch who, from on high, issues marching orders to the Church. The recent conciliar insistence on the collegial nature of the episcopacy and the communal nature of the Church (reflected in such metaphors as pilgrimage and body of Christ) has done much to lay to rest the notion of the Church being ruled by an absolute monarch. As that has happened, our understanding of the role and symbolic function of the papacy must also change. At its very best the contemporary understanding of the papacy would be something like this: Catholics today look to Peter to articulate its deepest and most universal faith, to express the needs of the entire Church, to exercise a prophetic ministry to the world in the name of the Church, to give expression to, and to guard, the unity of the Church and, last but not least, to listen, and give voice to, the needs and aspirations of the faithful as a whole. Peter, in short, serves the whole Church.

To exercise such a ministry means that the papacy can no longer be a one way street with orders coming from above to those below. It means, in essence, that the Pope as servant must be seen in dialogue with the Church. The Pope must learn as well as instruct since the Church is both a learning and a teaching Church. If the older model of the Church was a pyramid with the Pope at the apex, the new model is more like a wheel with the Pope at the hub.

Such a model of the papacy does not mean that it should function merely as a kind of "clearing house" for the current state of Catholic opinion. It does not envision the Pope as a kind of chairman of an ongoing discussion group. Such a model would be to hopelessly vulgarize the function of the Pope as it has been traditionally understood. It does mean that the Pope ought to reflect in his ministry the very best perception of what the Church is and what it aspires to be at a given moment in its history. The papacy ought to be a moral presence and it must be a check against those who would like to universalize the pretensions of a particular Church or a given tradition; it must be, in short, a universal ministry. Finally, it must be a locus of both encouragement and warning to the world in the name of the Gospel. Its prophetic function must be above the foreign policy of various countries or the purely practical consequences of particular ideologies. In practical terms, this means that if a Pope speaks on an issue which grates against, say, the reigning verities of this country the question must be not whether the Pope is anti-American, but whether the American (or African or whatever) verities are in tension with the understanding of the Gospel.

To put into practice such a policy means, inevitably, that the Pope will be a sign of contradiction to many and diverse local constituencies both in and outside the Church. That should not come either as a source of scandal or a surprise. The Gospel, after all, has many "hard sayings" which are meant precisely to catch us off guard and cause us to re-examine (or examine for the first time) who and what we are in the light of the Gospel.

The Petrine Ministry as Ecumenical Problem

It has long been recognized by even the most casual reader of the history of Christianity that the papacy is *the* stumbling block for those Christian bodies who seek a closer relationship with the Roman Catholic Church. That fact derives from the Catholic understanding of papal primacy and, more particularly, papal infallibility. Beyond those doctrinal formulations is the long-standing suspicion, born from historical circumstances, about the Pope and all that his office implies for those who are not Catholic. Those suspicions can range from the virulent anti-Catholic prejudice of those who cry "No popery!" to the less impassioned but real concerns of ecumenically minded Christians who are not unsympathetic to the Catholic Church.

The problem of the papacy is not one that is going to go away by simply wishing that it was not a problem. We need to state at the beginning that the papacy is intimately tied to Catholic self-definition and must be recognized as such. Most Catholics, one suspects, do not feel oppressed by the papacy or subservient to its dictates even if within Catholicism there is a willingness to contest certain papal actions or call for certain papal reforms. Most Catholics feel that what gives them their peculiar identity is a certain bond with the ancient Church of Rome. Those who express themselves on this issue, even when they may be critical of the papacy, feel that the absence of the papacy would severely diminish, if not fatally wound, the sense of being a Catholic. Hans Küng, as persistent a Catholic critic of the papacy as one can name, has written with some passion on this issue:

> Perhaps the Eastern Orthodox or Protestant Christian will be able to sympathize a little with the Catholic in his conviction that something would be lacking in his church and perhaps in Christendom as a whole if this Petrine ministry were suddenly to disappear; something that is not inessential to the church. How much it would mean for Christendom if this ministry were freshly understood dispassionately and unsentimentally in the light of Holy Scripture as what it ought to be: service to the church as a whole.*

The common ecumenical attempt to restate the role of the papacy in the context of the Christian Church has been going on apace. Since the conclusion of the Second Vatican Council high level theological exchanges between Roman Catholic and non-Catholic scholars have included long discussions on the papacy. Those theologians are not instructed to paper over real points of tension between the traditions. Their task is to discover what genuine points of agreement and concord can be affirmed as a first step to a greater sense of unity among the churches. The progress at the theological level among the discussants has been great. Let me cite just one example: the agreements reached by a task force of Roman Catholic and Lutheran scholars on the issue of the papacy:

> In these sessions we have once again found common ground. There is a growing awareness among Lutherans of the necessity of a specific ministry to serve the church's unity and universal mission, while Catholics increasingly see the need for a more nuanced understanding of the role of the papacy within the universal church.

---

*Hans Küng, *On Being a Christian* (Garden City: Doubleday, 1976), p. 500.

Lutherans and Catholics can now begin to envision possibilities of concord, and to hope for solutions to problems that have previously seemed insoluble. We believe that God is calling our churches to draw closer together, and it is our prayer that this joint statement on papal primacy may make some contribution to that end.*

It is one thing for theologians to find points of contact; it is quite another for practical efforts to flow from such discussions. The possibility of actual agreements between Catholics and Orthodox, Episcopalian, Lutheran, and other Christian bodies is there, but many issues need further clarification and study. It is the willingness to engage in such discussions that is the most encouraging aspect of the whole enterprise, especially since there is the possibility for practical things to flow from such discussions. In this period, we can only add that ordinary "in the pew" Catholics should also strive to deepen their own sense of the Petrine ministry as part of their life as Catholics.

We need to affirm without apologies that the papacy is part of our experience of being Catholics. Peter's successor represents our sense of tradition, our convictions about apostolicity, our clearest and most visible sign of unity, as well as the focus of our claims of universality. At the same time, we must also resist viewing the Pope as some kind of divine oracle or an absolute—however benign—spiritual dictator who "heads up" the Church. We find our unity in the Church founded on the apostolic college with Peter's successor holding preeminent place.

At the practical level of every-day Catholic living we need be sensitive to the office of the papacy and open to learning from it (as well as teaching it) since it represents the entire Church. In the eucharistic prayer we mention both the Pope and the local bishop by name. Most of us hear that prayer invoked almost automatically. What we should try to think of as we pray for the bishop and the Pope is that we belong to a community which is larger than *my* parish and even *my* diocese; we belong to a universal community of believers.

The current ecumenical discussions about the papacy (and related issues) remind us that we have a responsibility for healing the divisions in the Christian world. We will have more to say about our relationship to other churches in the ensuing pages. Here, at least, we should note

---

*Paul Empie and T. Austin Murphy, eds., *Papal Primacy and the Universal Church: Lutherans and Catholics in Dialogue IV* (Minneapolis: Augsburg, 1974), p. 10.

that it is a duty not to make the papacy into a stumbling block for others by inflating its claims beyond what doctrinal tradition demands. Excessive papalism, too frequently expressed, is a chauvinism that is more social than religious and harms the Church immensely. Catholics do not need, nor should they be subjected to, loyalty tests. Too often such loud protestations of fidelity to the Pope are, beneath the surface, simply a club with which to threaten critics in the Church who do not share the narrow concerns of the wielder.

Structure and Dissent

We have insisted throughout this chapter that the Petrine ministry is, first and foremost, a visible sign of the unity of the Church. Most older Catholics can attest that, except for the most trivial or innocuous matters, it was once unthinkable to openly dissent from the teaching authority of either the Pope or the bishops of the Church. That does not seem to be the case today. One need only scan the papers or watch television regularly to see that there are open tensions in the Church over a wide variety of issues. Politicized clergy hold public office in defiance of the wishes of the Vatican; Catholics, both clerical and lay, openly question the Church on matters of sexual morality; others refuse to implement the liturgical reforms of the Church; certain theologians seem to be in confrontation with the Vatican; people have openly challenged the papacy on a range of issues from the ordination of women to the utility of liberation theology. The once docile and obedient Church seems to be in a turmoil of dissent and discussion. Such turmoil is generated both from the ultra conservatives of the right and the revisionists of the left.

Somehow we need to make sense of this dissent and tension while keeping in focus our affirmations about the organic unity of the Church and its relationship to the successor of Peter who is, we affirm, the visible head of the Church. How do we account for this dissent and how do we respond to it? Let us personalize the problem a bit. Suppose, at our hypothetical parish, the pastor reads a letter from the bishop on some particular issue (abortion, nuclear arms, world peace . . . pick the issue) about which we have passionate convictions contrary to what the bishop states. Indeed, on a matter like birth control, we might not only disagree but see the matter as an issue of personal integrity or one that involves life or death decisions for us personally. How do we react in such circumstances so that we keep in balance our respect for the teaching Church and our own sense of personal conscience?

At this point we might keep some important distinctions in mind. There are a number of questions which are more or less a matter of policy and which involve purely disciplinary matters; those are issues where there is no basic doctrinal question at stake. For example, there is a rather silly rule from Rome which forbids girls and women from serving (never mind, presiding) at the altar. That is a disciplinary regulation without doctrinal content. Or the matter may be one of long-standing tradition (e.g. celibacy of the clergy) but, again, not doctrinally central to the faith. On issues like this it seems not only possible but, within the limits of courtesy, desirable that discussion should take place. Articulated dissent in such areas is a good therapy to ward off the pretensions of power or the guardianship of privilege which often afflict historical organizations. On some issues it might even become an issue of "doing justice" to dissent. For example: the desirability of a celibate clergy is a legitimate area of dispute while the prohibition of female altar servers seems to be an example of petty injustice which ought to be contested. The Church, after all, is not free from such injustices (and never will be) because the Church is always in the process of being reformed and will always need reform until the *eschaton* arrives.

But suppose the tension or dissent is framed in terms of an issue where it is alleged that essential truths of the Church are at stake? What are we to say about those instances where there is a gap between what someone professes (either singly or as a group) and what the official Church professes? What criterion do we use for resolving such tensions? Some words that the late G. K. Chesterton wrote a half century ago seem to me useful still; he is speaking about the charge that Chaucer's bitter criticisms of the Church sounded very much like the language of the heretical Lollards of the same period. Chesterton writes:

> A man does not come an inch nearer to being a heretic by being a hundred times a critic. Nor does he do so because his criticisms resemble those of critics who are also heretics. He only becomes a heretic at the precise moment when he prefers his criticism to his Catholicism; that is, at the instant of separation in which he thinks

the view peculiar to himself more valuable than the creed that unites him to his fellows.*

There is a good deal of wisdom in Chesterton's observation. In our age, when information is easily obtainable and the level of education high, it is not surprising that people are more probing and more critical in their judgments. A good deal of dissent in the Church comes from the pluralism of contemporary culture, the more democratic spirit of the age, the rise of civil rights, and the not surprising reaction of many in the Church against the real or perceived rigidities of the past. We cannot even list all of the issues which stir up dissent and/or discontent in the Church today, but we can set down a legitimate basic principle that stands before any issue: when dissent reaches the point where the basic fabric of ecclesial unity is breached, that dissent becomes immoral in the sense that Chesterton describes it; it becomes a glorification of the self at the expense of the self-forgetting love which, at its base, energizes the community of believers. The New Testament itself bears eloquent testimony to the problems and dissensions of the early Church. Such dissent is behind a good deal of what is written, say, in the Acts of the Apostles. The New Testament, at the same time, exhorts to unity, laments tendencies to schism, and resists mightily the temptation to sectarian separation. The most treacherous aspect of dissent turned into heresy is its power to rend the seamless garment of Christ in the name of a partial (or deformed) truth which is seen as total and non-negotiable.

The Church is less inclined to thunder out anathemas or level charges of heresy today than it was in the past. In fairness, we must admit that the Church is much more open to dialogue, to discussion, and to mediation. That is, in itself, a very good and hope-filled sign of the times. The "official" Church must remain open to those experiences. The dissenters, on the other hand, must also be ready to test their dissent according to a broad view of the Church: Does this dissent advance the Gospel in the world and does it do so with evident concern for both Christian charity and Christian unity? When those boundaries are breached there is a good case for the invocation of the term heresy.

---

*G. K. Chesterton, *Chaucer* (London: Faber and Faber, 1932), pp. 249–50.

A recent theological understanding of heresy makes the point with conviction:

> . . . heresy ought only to designate the unwillingness to listen, to be open. Mistakes can be corrected with education, openness, and patience. But a basic closure to God's word, manifested by obstinacy, deceit, and intolerance, can only be corrected by conversion. The struggle to obtain clarity does not destroy communion but smugness will do it every time . . . heresy comes from a deep closed-mindedness to revelation and symbolizes a concealment of divine truth (which is, secondarily, expressed by erroneous beliefs and self absorbed lifestyles).*

Living with Structures

Today we often hear of people who still consider themselves as Catholics but rarely go to church or who define themselves as Catholics but "not very good ones." Just as often we met people who, without fanfare, simply drift away from the Church into a kind of religious limbo. When people tell us—often this is unsolicited information—that they are "not very good" Catholics or, ruefully, "fallen-away" Catholics, they are manifesting a good deal of dissatisfaction, if at a passive level, with the Church as an institution. It is not a rare phenomenon. Large structures, whether civil or religious, can be a real source of alienation for people. Many alienated Catholics express a kind of rebellion. It may be a passive rebellion, against an institution which they see as more concerned with itself than with the needs of the individual. Every person in the Church must confess in all honesty that not every "fallen-away" Catholic is acting in bad faith or from false consciousness. The "fallen-away" or the "drifted-away" stands as a powerful symbol of accusation. It is one of the lamentable facts of life that the very institution that defines itself as the trustee of Christ's revelation can also act as an anti-sign of Christ for people. To think otherwise is to impute to the Church an angelic existence which it does not have, and has never claimed to possess.

With that observation in mind, however, we need to say clearly that to be a Christian is to be called into community. All religion is, by

---

*William E. Reiser, *What Are They Saying About Dogma?* (Ramsey: Paulist, 1978), pp. 84–85.

its nature, social. While a person may rightly feel that his or her faith is an intimately personal affair it is also a plain fact of history that faith must find outlet in social forms. Christianity demands personal conversion to Christ and aversion from sin. But that converted person, in Christ, is part of his mystical body. The Church of the Acts of the Apostles sets the standard for the Church: "They devoted themselves to the apostles' teaching and fellowship, to the breaking of bread and the prayers" (Acts 2:42).

How does one live in the Church? With a serene conviction that it is there that we can hear God's word proclaimed and his body and blood celebrated. With the full understanding that the Church will never be more perfect or more pure or more loving than the people (like us) who make it up. With the conviction that the Church, as a community of memory, holds on to the graces, the resources, and the models to help us in the following of Christ.

Why does one remain in the Church? For at least two very good reasons. First, because it is in the Church that we perceive—however dimly at times—that it is there that we can receive, grow in, and be nurtured by, the reality of Christ. Second, because we are the Church, and our absence—any absence—diminishes the people of God not just numerically (hardly important) but spiritually. Let us reiterate that final second point: we are Catholics not only because in the Church we have access and resources that help us grow in Christ but also because we have *obligations* to build the body of Christ. To paraphrase St. Paul: it is our task to build up those things which are lacking in the body of Christ.

Points for Discussion

(a) What is your own image of the Pope as you perceive him as head of the Church? What kind of reactions do you experience to his image?

(b) Are there things that the Pope has done/said to which you have personally responded (either negatively or positively) as a religious person?

(c) What do you see as the most urgent matters which demand reform in the Church?

(d) Do you have a strong sense of being a Catholic who is a *Roman* Catholic?

(e) What qualities/virtues, charismas do you think are most needed in the papacy? Could you sketch out what you think would be an ideal profile of a contemporary Pope?

Chapter VI

Becoming Catholic

To be a Christian is to profess faith in Jesus the Christ who is model, Savior, and Lord; to be a Catholic is to profess that Christian faith in a particular and definable tradition. Being Catholic, then, is not merely "joining" a church the way one might join a social club or a sorority or a political party. Being a Catholic, as we have already insisted, is to undertake a journey, both personal and social, in the company of Jesus the Christ. It is true, as we have already observed, that people are Catholic by accident of birth or by reason of their culture or nationality. But to become a Catholic or to be a Catholic in the religious sense is not an accomplished fact; it is an aspiration, an undertaking, and a life-long journey.

Being Catholic means to live in a certain way. The burden of this chapter will be to explore the ways in which a person in the Catholic tradition lives out his or her religious faith. In a very rough way we want to explore the manner in which a Catholic receives and expresses his or her faith. We shall affirm that at the root of the Catholic experience is the participation in the sacramental life of the Church and in the ministry of the Church. These two concepts—ministry and sacrament—are intimately connected but need to be considered, for the sake of clarity, in turn.

Sacramental Life

The traditional catechism defined a sacrament as an "outward sign instituted by Christ to give grace." That definition was meant to explicate the traditional seven sacraments (baptism, confirmation, penance, Holy Eucharist, anointing of the sick, matrimony, and holy orders) of the Church. In a broader sense, however, that same definition can stand for a larger reality and a more generous understanding of the word "sacrament." We can call that larger notion the *basic sacramentality* of the Church. Basic sacramentality means that Catholicism has a deep conviction that God's gracious presence is mediated to us through visible realities. Christ is, of course, the visible reality *par excellence*. Christ is the visible and real sign of God's concern for the world. The Church, in turn, is also a visible sign, willed by Christ, to give grace to the world through other visible signs, gestures, and other perceivable realities which signal the continuing work of Christ in the world.

The traditional gestures of the Church—the seven sacraments— parallel the human development of a person as the medieval theologians loved to note. In that sense the sacraments are signposts of our earthly pilgrimage. Parents bring their infants to the baptismal font to signify their acceptance by the Christian community. When children are a bit older they are admitted to the rites of Holy Communion, they may approach the sacrament of penance for the forgiveness of sin, and they are strengthened (i.e. confirmed) in their baptismal conviction by the sacrament of confirmation which is baptism's natural adjunct. When people set out in a new manner of social existence the Church celebrates their rites of marriage. At the crises of their life, especially those which threaten life itself, the Church prays with them and anoints them with gestures of hope for their health and recovery in spirit and body.

Beyond these mile-post moments of birth, growth, change, and bodily danger there are those constant celebrations of the Eucharist which are effective signs of Catholic unity, worship, and the communal desire to hear the word of God and share in the sacramental reality of Christ in communion. As we have insisted throughout this book it is in those sacramental celebrations that we find the most profound sense of the Christian life in the Catholic tradition.

These sacramental signs of the "great sign" which is the Church do not exhaust the visible gestures which the Church makes use of to make Christ visible and tactile to the world. The sacraments are celebrated in time and space, and it is in those realities—place and time— that we see Christ enter and penetrate our world and our consciousness.

The great moments—birth, personal growth, marriage, illness and so on—are sacramentalized in the Catholic tradition. Almost every religious tradition one can name has similar rites to celebrate these moments which the anthropologists call *rites of passage*. Even those who are non-religious feel the need to somehow solemnize the birth of a child, the coming of age of a young boy or girl, the act of marrying, and the mystery of death. These are peak moments and they reflect the wonder and mystery of human existence and human growth. The Church invests these moments with solemn import, and the solemnity is, naturally enough, linked to the saving mysteries of Christ.

This sacramental sense also impels the Church to assign a sign value to our experience of time. Our cycle of worship (the so-called "liturgical year") during the year celebrates the great mysteries of Christ in a special way. Any Catholic who has experienced the beauty of a Midnight Mass at Christmas or participated in the complex liturgy of the Easter Vigil understands that these are not ordinary times. They are special moments carrying a great freight of meaning. They are times in which we step outside of the ordinary rhythms of life in order to enter into the central mysteries of our faith.

In a more informal way the Church also celebrates with us those other "special" times which mark our lives. With prayer and ritual we commemorate anniversaries, pray together during a tragedy, honor a graduation, give thanks for peace and bounty, and mourn with those who suffer. All of those acts of worship—many done for an *ad hoc* occasion—can be considered as sacramental in the true sense of the term.

These special and solemn moments illustrate a deep conviction of the Church: that our ordinary life as lived is intermingled with, and punctuated by, an awareness of those special times which are freighted with the presence of Christ. Not all of us have a keen sense of "Christian" time (the slow evolution of Sunday from the Lord's day to being part of the "weekend" has changed all that), but the resources—in the form of Sunday worship, holy days, special events in one's religious life—are there to aid us to recollect Christ's presence in our midst.

Besides the more special and public temporal observances of the Church are those other sign-moments which are more private or familial in nature. Many of these sign-moments are so common and so much a part of custom that only rarely do we reflect on their significance: those brief prayers before meals, the prayers lisped by children before they tuck in for the night, etc. These gestures and moments are small ways in which we—often without a great deal of explicit advertence—transform the mundane into the holy. When, for example, we say grace before meals, we are saying, in effect, that we are dependent creatures and grateful ones. Those sentiments are expressed not only by the words but by the gestures we use (clasping the hands; bowing the head), and the fact that we *take the time* to perform such gestures.

Not only do we mark off time with sign-gestures but we do with the spaces we inhabit the very same thing. There is a deep human need to mark off undifferentiated space in order to make it "our" space.

When students move into a dormitory in which every room and all the furniture is exactly the same, the first thing that the students do is to distinguish their rooms (or parts of the room) with personal pictures, art works, possessions, etc. They create, in microcosm, a home. By analogy, we do the same thing with space in a religious sense. The simple act of placing a crucifix over a bed or hanging a religious picture on a wall is not only an act of faith (i.e. this house is inhabited by a believer) but is also an act of changing the character of the space. What we do in the privacy of home or office is done on a much larger scale by the Church. The Church, from its beginnings, has marked off certain sites (shrines, etc.) and built churches for sacred purposes, i.e. dedicated to the worship of God. It is, again, only with reflection that we see the significance of these sign-places. Every Sunday Catholics affirm their faith by the act of going from one place (their home) to go to another place (church) to worship. The movement from one place to another is significant in itself. We pass from our ordinary life in the home to the space of the church which has about it the air of a "sacred" place.* In that sacred place we utilize all kinds of symbolic gestures and body language. We use certain symbolic gestures (bowing, kneeling, etc.), observe silence, and, ordinarily, dress in a festive or serious manner.

To celebrate the mysteries of Christ at certain times in certain places is one of the hallmarks of the Catholic sacramental sense of relationship to God. The simple act of going to church on Sunday is a sign-gesture which signals our belief in the reality of a transcendental dimension of our ordinary life. This is not mere sentimentality. The marking off of time and space responds to a profound human instinct. The entire sacramental life of the Church can be seen in the context of the celebration of certain times in certain places. When, in my classes, I have asked students to describe their ideal wedding, they often say that they want to get married in a certain church. When I inquire why this or that parish, they will often reply that because there they went to church, were baptized, made their First Communion, were confirmed, and so on. What they are saying, without being able to articulate it, is that a good deal of who they are religiously is defined by certain important peak moments in their lives: their sense of the parish is that it

---

*It might be worth noting in passing that the word *profane* means, literally, the space outside the temple precincts.

affirmed for them their sense of faith as it is intertwined with their family, their own growth, their sense of tradition—their sense, in short, of what they are.

One must not exaggerate this consciousness, however. While certain vowed religious may have a keen sense of the sacred significance of time (they pray at fixed hours of the day and organize their life according to the liturgical year), most of us do not live in that fashion. Work, family, and so on dictate our organization of time. Going to Mass on Sunday may be a fractional part of our weekend living. We experience the moments of sacramentality in punctuated forms. To be fully Catholic means that we must become more reflective about those moments; we need to approach those moments and gestures with more attention. It is only then that we will fully realize that being a Catholic is not a static state but an ever growing process of awareness.

Sacramentality and Life

The liturgical/sacramental life is not the sum total of what it means to be a Catholic. It is one of the oldest clichés in Christianity to say that what one professes on Sunday ought to be put into practice on Monday. Every cliché, however, is a repeated truth and this particular truth is flatly stated at the end of every liturgy:

> Priest: ''Go in peace to love and serve the Lord!''
> All: ''Thanks be to God.''

The great basic burden of Catholic life is to translate the gestures of faith and the prayers of observance into the texture of ordinary life in a fashion that actually makes a difference. That task is executed with exemplary clarity by the great saints and by the rest of us with varying degrees of enthusiasm, fervor, and success. It is one thing, for example, to affirm that we are at peace with one another in the liturgy and quite another to actually make peace with an obnoxious neighbor or a malicious relative. It is one thing to hear St. Paul's words about glorying in the cross of Christ and quite another to draw spiritual understanding and comfort from our personal burdens and trials.

It is, however, absolutely crucial to translate gesture into changed behavior. Catholicism, with its strong emphasis on the sacramental, is peculiarly prone to turning religious observance into a species of magic by which we manipulate gestures in order to get desired effects. There is a temptation to say—however subconsciously—that if I perform this act of devotion or attend that service, then everything will be all right.

It is not enough to go through the liturgical motions to be considered a Catholic. While Catholic theology says that the sacraments are effective *ex opere operato* (from the thing being done) it equally insists that one's intentions, resolutions, applications, and cooperation are what brings observance to its final goal of a closer life in Christ. One cannot mechanically go through the rites of penance if the basic intention of conversion is absent, just as one cannot marry without the intention of being married.

What all the above means in the concrete is that we must learn how to bridge the formal life of sacramental gesture and Church participation with the business of living. In Catholicism there is not a separate place for worship and ethics. The authentic response of faith works itself out in the way we are and the way we hope to be. When St. Augustine said "Love God and do as you please" he was not preaching moral anarchy; he put his finger on the very foundation of the Gospel: true faith, fully expressed, by its nature, spills over into the way one lives.

It is only when we begin to realize that a full participation in the sacramental life of the Church results in what the theologian Bernard Cooke calls "transformed experience" that we fully realize the intimate nexus between the life of worship and the life of acting and doing. Cooke writes:

> Christian life is sacramental. It is an experience that is thoroughly different because it has been transformed in its significance by the life, death, and resurrection of Jesus, the Christ. But it expresses that transformed meaning so that it can be communicated to others. Christians as individuals and in community bear witness to the "grace" of God's self-gift, and embody as sacrament this grace-giving revelation.*

How, in the practical order, do we make this connection between liturgy, sacramentality, and ordinary life? That is an enormously complex question worthy of volumes in its own right. There is one basic

---

*Bernard Cooke, *Sacraments and Sacramentality* (Mystic, Conn.: Twenty-Third Publications, 1983), p. 238. The *Journal of Religious Ethics* VII (1979) devotes an entire issue to the relationship of ethics and worship; it makes good reading on this subject.

point which we can insist upon: we need to cultivate a sense of *listening* in faith. So often in our religious life we do and we act, but when we worship, either in private devotional activities or by participation in the liturgy, we must listen as well as speak or act. It is one thing to hear the Gospel read out in church; it is quite another thing to *listen* to it. That listening is both a kind of openness or receptivity and a form of reflective questioning: What does this text say to me? Why am I making this gesture? What do the words, recited almost by rote, actually signify as they are said at the beginning of each meal? To cultivate that contemplative and questioning form of listening brings, almost inevitably, further questions of action: How do I love my neighbor? What does it really mean to take up a cross? In what concrete manner do I actually think of myself as a thankful person? How do I actually seek out the will of God?

It is only in those moments of reflective listening (listening is my term for being open to the impulses of God's grace) that those things which are mechanical and/or routine in my religious life take on personal significance, urgency, and power. We must be aware of the possibility that such listening may bring with it great demands on our comfortable way of life. Francis of Assisi had heard the Gospel read out at Mass all of his life but only one day when he *listened* to the Gospel admonition to live poorly did he walk out of the church and begin to live a life of radical poverty. In the case of Francis the word of God did penetrate like a two-edged sword. Most of us, I suspect, would shrink from a conversion that dramatic, but all of us, unless we are going through the religious motions, need listen not only to words but to gestures and signs. It is in that listening, after all, that we begin to sense the word of God.

A final point: our listening must not dwell on the cosmic level. To pray "for the world" or to seek the "conversion of the nations" or to ask for succor for the "poor of Africa" is fine, but it can often lead us to a kind of complacency: let God in his wisdom accomplish this or that. The authentic listener is the one who begins with the obligations closest to him or her while remaining open to what God leads us to. Mother Teresa of Calcutta was a nun for over twenty years when one day on a train in India she "saw" the poor of India by really looking at them for the first time. She did not set out to then save the world. She just began to help the dying destitute of Calcutta. And God supplied the rest.

Ministry

In the documents of the Second Vatican Council there is reaffirmed a distinction which is ancient in the Church, a distinction between those who are sacramentally ordained to ministry (the three sacramentally ordained offices are bishop, priest, and deacon) and the laity who share in the prophetic, priestly, and kingly function of Christ not as ordained ministers but to "carry out their own part in the mission of the whole Christian people with respect to the Church and the world."* That distinction between clergy and laity has immensely wide ramifications for understanding the Church.

There was a tendency to think of "ministers" in the Church as being those who were either sacramentally ordained or those who were in religious vows (monks, nuns, brothers, etc.) as opposed to those who were in the lay state. In fact, the Second Vatican Council distinguishes the laity by saying that they are those who are not in sacred orders or in religious vows.** The popular notion was that the clergy and religious were the "professionals" who "ran" things in the Church or, better, who were in charge of all ministerial functions. That rather common notion requires a good deal of modification. A certain number of observations are in order.

First, we must distinguish the office of the episcopacy and the priesthood and their development over the long history of the Church. It is the essential function of the bishop (the word means an overseer) to preside over a part of the Church, to preach the word, and to celebrate the Eucharist. The priests exercise the very same ministry under the authority of the bishop. The bishop is an overseer of a part of the Church and the priest is his extension. The ministry of preaching, teaching, presiding over the Eucharist and guiding a part of the Church pertains to the essence of the episcopal office.

Over the long haul of history, however, a vast and complicated episcopal and sacerdotal culture grew up. The story of that development is far too complex to trace, but it should be noted that as a part of that culture the clergy (my shorthand term here for bishops and priests) began to wear distinctive clothes, were not free to marry (except in the Eastern Church where priests, but not bishops, may marry), lived in special residences, observed certain religious duties not obligatory of

---

*The Dogmatic Constitution on the Church, IV.31, in Documents, p. 57.
**Ibid.

the laity, etc. The point to be emphasized is that all of these developments are historical in their nature and do not pertain to the essence of the episcopal or sacerdotal office. They could be modified, changed, or abolished tomorrow without harm to the essence of what it means to be a bishop or a priest.

Deacons are an order of service. Deacons (some married men today are ordained to this office but, as yet, women are not) may baptize, preach, bring Communion to the sick, and otherwise serve the needs of the local church. Traditionally the diaconate was seen as a step to the priesthood but, as we noted, today deacons can be permanent ministers at that rank. This change occurred after the Second Vatican Council when the Council expressed a desire for the restoration of the permanent diaconate, thus restoring what had been the usage of the ancient Church.

The offices of the bishop, priest, and deacon constitute what is called the hierarchy of the Church. They constitute the clergy. Along with the clergy are those male and female religious who profess public vows (usually of poverty, chastity, and obedience). In their vowed life they either serve the Church in the active apostolate of teaching, tending the sick and so on or as contemplatives who devote themselves to prayer and meditation. The religious life is a significant part of Catholicism, and this way of life, as the Second Vatican Council said, is of "unsurpassing value" to the Church.*

Does the sacramental office of the hierarchy and the vowed life of the religious exhaust all of the ministerial possibilities in the Church? By no means. And that brings us to our second point. Just as all are called to Christ in the Church, so all are called to the building up of that Church and its extension in time and space. It is basic to Catholic belief that every baptized Christian is called upon to minister to the Church and to the world. While the Church insists on the theological distinction between clergy and laity, it would be false to conclude that there is a distinction between those who are called to minister and those who are not called.

But how do we all minister?

It would be impossible to even list the various ministries in the Church much less describe them. We can set out five models of ministry which Bernard Cooke, in an authoritative study, has proposed.**

---

*Decree on the Appropriate Renewal of the Religious Life, I.1, in Documents, p. 467.

**Bernard Cooke, *Ministry to Word and Sacrament: History and Theology* (Philadelphia: Fortress, 1976).

Cooke says that if one examines the Christian tradition, all ministry seems oriented to (1) the formation of community, (2) God's word, (3) service to the people of God, (4) God's judgment, and (5) the sacraments of the Church. It should be clear even from this rudimentary listing that clergy, religious, and laity all participate in those ministries, or, to put it differently, no one of these ministries is the exclusive province of one or the other.

If we go back and take a look at our hypothetical parish we see examples of all these five kinds of ministry taking place—the ministries being exercised by both ordained and non-ordained ministers. As I write these words I have before me on my desk the bulletins of a few local parishes. In glancing over their terse announcements I see the exercise of every kind of ministry outlined by Cooke: the usual schedule of Masses, baptisms, and confessions (5) is followed by a list of newly inscribed parishioners to be visited in their homes (1) while the bulletins also announce Bible study classes and other classes of religious enrichment both for parishioners and interested non-Catholics (2). There are social action committee meetings to be called to discuss strategies both to fight abortion and to protest capital punishment (4) as well as a request for goods for the needs of the St. Vincent de Paul Society and announcements of visitations of local hospitals and nursing homes (3). All of these organized activities are manned by people who *minister*, i.e. they read the Scriptures, visit the sick, help the needy, teach catechism, celebrate the liturgy and sacraments, and give witness about issues which concern the consciences of the Catholic.

Every Catholic reader will recognize those ministries and be able to add to the list. Something as banal as a close reading of a parish bulletin (or the most innocuous of Catholic magazines) illustrates the widely diverse ministries which fall under Professor Cooke's large headings. What is not often appreciated, save upon some reflection, is how much history and continuity stands behind those various ministries and how they have changed over time. A generation ago—and less— it was unheard of to have a lay person read the Scriptures from the altar at the Sunday Mass and unthinkable that a layperson would distribute Communion at Mass or take it to the sick or shut-ins at their homes or in the hospital. That is done today in most parishes. On the other hand the works of charity have often been in the hands of lay people. The parish St. Vincent de Paul Society, for example, is part of a movement which was started by the French scholar and lay activist, Antoine Frederic Ozanam (1813–1853), early in the last century.

What all ministerial activities have in common is the conviction that the presence of Christ should be made manifest and concrete in our world. Hence all ministry is, in the deepest sense of the term, sacramental. The impulse "to do" is energized by the deeper desire "to be" Christian and in that being to both imitate Christ more fully and to expand the presence of Christ to others. Ministries are ends in themselves only to the degree that they make real and present Christ in time and space, which is, after all, the task entrusted to the Church as a whole. That making present of the reality of Christ, then, becomes the sole and authentic criterion that the Church uses for establishing ministries in the Church.

When we stress the continuity of Christian ministry we should not do it as an excuse for forgetting the needs for new forms of ministry suited to the times and condition of particular epochs. The history of the Church is replete with examples of new and radical kinds of ministry that arise according to changing circumstances. When urban life began to increase in the Middle Ages, for example, the Franciscan movement was born in an attempt to touch the masses who were no longer ministered to by the more place-bound monasteries of an earlier period. In the famous aphorism of Chesterton, "What Benedict stored, Francis scattered." Similarly, the Dominicans were founded for the primary purpose of preaching the Gospel at every level of urban society from the university pulpit to the public square. In the seventeenth century there was an explosion of new religious orders and new kinds of lay confraternities to meet the challenges posed both by the Protestant Reformation and the expanding horizons triggered by European exploration and colonization. In our own century—think of Catholic Action, Cursillo, *Opus Dei*, Marriage Encounter, charismatic groups, The Catholic Workers, The Little Sisters and Brothers of Charles de Foucauld, etc.—new kinds of experiments in ministry have been tried to fit the peculiar needs of our time.

Ministry always reflects the tension (and it is usually a creative tension) between the inherited past and the demands of the new. Someone like a Mother Teresa of Calcutta exercises a ministry of charity which is as old as Catholicism itself. Were one to transport this remarkable woman back in time she would be doing the very same thing as she does today. On the other hand, the Dominican sister in our parish who serves as a hospital chaplain is engaged in a new kind of ministry just as much as the retired school teacher who is a permanent deacon. Their ministries only became possible because of the shifts in the post-Vatican II Church. They do what a generation ago priests did but with the diminution of priests and a redefinition of their ministry new kinds of ministries have arisen to take their place.

Prophetic Witness

In the biblical parlance a *prophet* is one who speaks with the authority of God. A prophet may speak about the future (which is what we normally take a prophetic task to be) but, in the Hebrew sense of the term, the prophet is an announcer of God's word. That explains why so many of the chapters in the books of the prophets begin with phrases like "Thus says the Lord . . ." or "The word of God to the prophet . . ." The prophets of the Old Testament spoke to the children of Israel to teach, to reprove, to call them back to the fidelity of the covenant, and, at times, to hold out the promise of the messianic future. Jesus' manner of speaking and teaching was such that many in his audience took him to be a prophet. Jesus did share—among other things—one thing in common with the ancient prophets: his words were often received with great hostility by the crowds, a hostility which would lead eventually to his death.

The strength of prophetic speech and prophetic activity comes from the tension between what the prophet says and what the audience wants, or does not want, to hear. The Christian message can be a source of immense solace to us in our need but it can also be a major irritant to us in our periods of complacency and self-satisfaction. We simply do not enjoy hearing about forgiveness when we are in a vengeful mood or suffering some injustice, just as we do not want to hear about the cross or self-denial when we are finally enjoying some status of pleasure or well-being. The plain fact of the matter is that there is a good deal in the Gospels which makes a hash of our comfortable assumptions and our more egotistical desires. The very quasi-religious comfort we possess from being a member of a comfortable parish hearing our friend the pastor saying words made comfortable by their repetition (after all, we've been hearing them all of our lives) is one way in which there is erected—even if at an unconscious level—a barrier against the word of

God. It is all so easy—for all of us—to become creatures of religious habit.

The prophetic ministry of the Church is exercised by those who pierce those comfortable barriers and make us uncomfortable enough to once again rehear the Gospel in such a way that our present life is altered or put off-center. Prophetic speech is not the special provenance of any class in the Church. One is not ordained a prophet. Prophetic speech arises when someone has an insight into the Gospel that is compelling enough for that person to speak in the name of the Gospel even if that speaker is a minority of one. Thus, by a prophetic impulse, a humble laywoman like St. Catherine of Siena (1347–1380) could reprove the action of Popes and demand of them that they return from their residence in France and again take up residence in the city of Rome. Thus, also, but in a different manner, the very life of a Saint Francis of Assisi (1181?–1226) could serve as a prophetic reproach to the wealth and laxity of medieval society in general and the Church in particular. Examples of this kind of prophetic speech and action occur in every age of the Church's life.

It would be comforting to report that it is easy to spot prophetic speech and customary to respond to it. Alas, the contrary is true, for, to paraphrase Jesus in the Gospel, the prophet is rarely recognized in his own time and place. With the gap of historical hindsight we can praise the boldness of a Catherine or the moral beauty of a Francis but their contemporaries were quick to dismiss Catherine as a "mouthy woman" and Francis as a "ragged fanatic." To distinguish the true prophet from the simple nag or the obsessed neurotic is not always easy. In fact, the prophet, more often than not, merely upsets us or provokes rage. At that stage we may merely be called upon to pose a counter-argument. But, even in that simple response, the prophet forces us to think about things we do not want to think about.

I would like to give two widely diverse examples of possibly prophetic speech made in our own time, not to assure the reader that they are prophetic, but to help us understand how possibly prophetic speech pulls us up short.

(a) In a series of sermons delivered in 1984 Pope John Paul II not only vigorously defended the traditional Catholic ban on artificial contraception (which reaffirmed Paul VI's now famous encyclical *Humanae Vitae*) but argued that the prohibition rests on a fundamental understanding of Christian marriage. It is a position that many Catholics do not want to hear and, indeed, most will not hear. It flies in the face of the beliefs of Catholics (and, judging by polls, their practice), it is a scandal to non-Catholics, and it seems cruel in the face of population problems. The issue is this: Is this vigorous defense based, as the critics would have it, on a desire to reassert papal authority, or is it, never mind how unpopular, a crucial but forgotten teaching about the nature of marital love and human sexuality? Were the papal sermons simply reactionary in nature or were they prophetic utterances made to a complacent world? At the very least, for those who read or heard them, there came an occasion in which thinking about marriage and sexuality had to be confronted within the context of the Church.

(b) A small but vocal number of lay and clerical Catholics have argued that all cooperation with, or connection to, the modern nuclear armaments industry is radically immoral and directly antagonistic to the spirit of Jesus. People should not only resist cooperating with such an industry but should take action against it at least through vocal and dramatic protests. Many people (at least in this country) not only reject that argument but turn from it as a position closely tied to treachery. They argue for the needs of national defense and dismiss the critics as utopian cranks or self-absorbed fanatics. Both sides of this argument, from the perspective of their membership in the Church, must ultimately test their position against the reading of the Gospel.

In both of the cases mentioned above, the utterances, made in the name of the Gospel, are in direct conflict with what the majority feels. The utterances are not only not accepted but they provoke strong reactions from the hearers. Who is right in these issues? That is hard to say since prophets only get vindicated in time. Empirically speaking, it will only be future generations who will be able to say, amid the shambles of family life for example, that the Pope was right. If the nuclear activists are right, alas, there may be no future generations to pass judgment.

Prophetic utterances may be directed to the Church from within the Church or by those in the Church directed to the larger world. We are mainly concerned here with prophetic utterances to the Church. We need to remind ourselves that in history the Church is as fragile as its members and, as such, must always be called back to repentance: *ecclesia semper reformanda*. The prophetic tradition does for the Church what it once did for Israel: call people back to fidelity to the covenant with God. The Church, as the bearer of the good news, must also speak to the larger world. It is, after all, the basic conviction of the Gospel that it has something "more" to add to the range of human experience and desire. The Church is most faithful to its task when it ministers to the world in time of great need; it is most faithless when it is silent when it should speak.

What is the connection between being Catholic and being attentive to prophetic witness? The connection rests in the basic stance of the Christian to be, in Karl Rahner's famous formulation, "hearers of the word." Being a Catholic means being open to the word as it is preached in church and taught and witnessed to in the confines of the community of all Catholics. We have never fully grasped God's word. We approach that word and seek to hear it and be faithful to it. The prophet, at the very least, reminds us of that responsibility of being a hearer. To shut off that word, no matter how jarring it might be to our sensibilities, is to freeze oneself in a state of spiritual immaturity when, in fact, we are called to maturity and fullness. The prophetic word in the Church—from whatever source it might come—invites us to go beyond what we are at present in order to become something else, to more fully "put on Christ." That is a primary vocation for every Christian. Rahner writes:

> To accept and to endure with patience and with trust in an even greater God and his grace the difference between what we are and what we should be is itself a positive task for Christians. A correct acceptance indeed always includes an attempt to overcome this difference in an upward direction, and hence it includes a "no" to something else and a "yes" to something else and better.*

The Scriptures enjoin us to be not only hearers of the word but doers of the word also. Our willingness to listen to God's word must be matched by our readiness to witness it in act. That doing of the word is part of the universal prophetic ministry of the Church. At a certain level everyone understands that, but at closer examination the theory gives way to the painful consequences of acting on what we have heard. We all "hear" the demand for justice to the poor, love for neighbor, conversion of life, taking up the cross, etc. We all agree that those are noble and desirable actions. The hearing of those injunctions, however, becomes difficult when we move them from the level of abstract in-

*Karl Rahner, *Foundations of Christian Faith* (New York: Seabury, 1978), pp. 407–08.

junctions to practical application, especially when those applications run contrary to our natural instincts, our sense of possession, our prejudices, and our sense of self-esteem. It is then that the prophetic voice becomes a reproach to us.

What is true of the individual is equally true of the Church as a whole. The Church has the task to preach and witness about those things which the world may find distasteful or even ludicrous. Nonetheless, the essence of prophetic ministry is to recognize the gap between what is and what should be. It is in bridging that gap that the sacramental/ministerial/prophetic task of the Church takes its legitimate place and finds its deepest legitimacy. The sacramental and prophetic tasks of the Church are not discrete. They form part of the indivisible whole of the Church's function.

It is one of the sad facts of Catholic reality that we tend to separate functions which ought to be seen—at least from one perspective—as a whole. It is contrary to Catholic life (even though there are good sociological and historical explanations for it) to leave the task of the Gospel to "professionals" who are either sacramentally ordained or vowed to religious life. It is an undeniable fact of Christianity that while there are separate functions and ministries in the Church there still exists, beyond those differentiations, a single people, called by God in Christ, who as an organic whole are called to witness to the reality, the pertinence, and the riches of Christ in the world.

Points for Discussion

(a) To what degree has the sacramental life of the Church played a part in the development of your own spiritual life?

(b) To what extent—if any—has your life been shaped by the Church and its celebrations? Are you enriched by the sacramental life of the Church?

(c) What do you consider to be the most powerful and meaningful ministries of the Church from the perspective of your own spiritual life? The weakest ministries?

(d) Are you aware of (and how have you responded to) prophetic utterances in the Church?

(e) What do you take to be your own contributions to the Church? How might you, under the most ideal of situations, minister in the Church?

Chapter VII

Catholicism as Worldview

T he title of this chapter may seem rather grandiose and ambitious, worthy of a volume in its own right. I have used the word *worldview* here for a rather precise reason and with a particular end in mind. One basic argument of this book is that being a Catholic is not like being a Democrat or a Rotarian; being a Catholic is not like being in an organization or joining a club. It is, rather, a mode of being in the world and, as such, it is a certain way of looking at the world from a particular point of view. That mode of being which is called Catholic should enhance a kind of seeing which, if not totally unique, is, at the very least, characteristic of Catholicism. That mode of being (and seeing) derives from both biblical roots and the peculiar understanding of those roots which have been a part of the long history and tradition of Catholicism in the world. As a consequence, the Catholic worldview shares with other Christian bodies (as well as Jewish, and, to a certain extent, Islamic ones) certain common themes and others which are more peculiar to itself.

Most of us who are not academic philosophers spend little time thinking about worldviews. We leave that to the professional thinkers. Nonetheless, even if we do not reflect on our basic understanding of the world, such an understanding is there. All of us "look out" at the world with a complex set of national, racial, temporal, family, and cultural presuppositions. We all view that world outside of ourselves from the vantage point of our own experiences and the limits put upon it.

What we will do in the following pages is to make explicit some of the underlying themes of Catholic experience in order to help ourselves grasp a bit better how a Catholic looks (or, better, ought to look) upon the world which is the proper arena of his or her activities.

The World as Gift

Every religious tradition attempts to account for the beginnings of the world and its meaning for people. Christianity is no exception. From its very beginnings the Christian Church has meditated upon the opening chapters of the Book of Genesis which deal with the beginnings

111

of the world. Since at least the middle of the last century there have been innumerable debates, most of them sterile and misplaced, about whether those first chapters of Genesis relate a "true" and "scientific" account of the world. I say these debates are misplaced because they are rather like asking if Orwell's *Animal Farm* is really about whether pigs can talk or not. It is to debate the wrong issue. We approach those pages to learn about God and the world; like St. Augustine, we pray, "Lord, open those pages to me."* The crucial question to ask of the Book of Genesis is this: What do those pages say about God's relationship to the world?

The Catholic tradition would answer unanimously that there are four basic irreducible truths to be learned from those pages; those four truths undergird a good deal of what the Church understands about the world.

(1) The world is not self-sufficient or self-explanatory. It was called into being (i.e. created) by a free and generous God.

(2) The world itself is not divine or sacred. It is a creation of God and is not to be identified with God. Unlike those who see the world as sacred—the traditional American Indians would be an example—the Book of Genesis makes a clear distinction between God and God's creation.

(3) The world, created by God, is a good one. At the end of each day in Chapter 1 of Genesis, God pronounced his handiwork as "good." The Genesis account stands in contrast to those philosophies and/or theologies which view the material world as evil or as an illusion holding one back from the sight of the Infinite.

(4) This world is the proper arena of human activity given to Adam and Eve (i.e. the primordial humans who represent all of the human race) as a gift. This free gift was one which was intended to be received in thanksgiving and held in stewardship.

Those four truths about the world and its relationship to people is at the core of the Christian understanding of creation and the world. It is the starting point for construction of the Catholic worldview. What is the response of humans to this series of basic biblical truths?

The primordial response to these truths should be a combination of wonder and gratitude. To look seriously at the world around us—

The Confessions, XI.2.

to really *see* the world—in the light of the teachings of the Book of Genesis is to begin developing a primary sense of gratitude not only for our existence but for the existence of the world itself which is our home. That sense of basic gratitude is the foundation stone of all spirituality. All attitudes of prayer, from adoration to the seeking of forgiveness, begins with the awareness that the world is, first and foremost, a good gift from God. While Catholicism balances its understanding of the goodness of God's world with doctrines about the sinful state of humanity and the need for salvation (doctrines rooted also in the Book of Genesis), it is still true that at the heart of Catholicism is a love for the world which is the first gift of God.

This sense of the world as coming from God manifests itself technically in the Catholic belief (vigorously denied by most of the early Protestant reformers) that people can come to a knowledge of the existence of God unaided by revelation. The First Vatican Council (1869–1870) taught this as an authentic part of Catholic teaching. The Council did not teach that every person did or could come to a knowledge of God's existence through reason. It did teach that humans have that capacity because "ever since the creation of the world his invisible nature, namely, his eternal power and deity, has been clearly perceived in the things that have been made" (Rom 1:20).

Why do we insist on this point? Not to argue that one can "reason" his or her way to God—it is basic to Christian doctrine that God speaks to us; we do not have to claw our way up to God—but to insist on a basic foundational point: our religious worldview is anchored in the reality and goodness of the created order as it comes from God. When we attempt to puzzle out our basic religious convictions in order to give them some cogency, we should not begin by looking up but by looking *around* us. Throughout its long history authentic Catholicism has had to struggle with various temptations to denigrate the world, temptations deriving from Platonism or various forms of dualism (e.g. the perfect world of spirit versus the evil world of matter) that despise the world around us as impediments to a true spirituality. We must insist that such temptations are pernicious and should be avoided. We belong in this world which comes from the hand of God. That sense of rootedness in the world is lovingly expressed in a prayer uttered by the bewildered hero of Walker Percy's novel *Love in the Ruins*. In a lucid moment in a hospital room after attempting suicide the hero cries out a near despairing prayer:

> Dear God, I see it now, why can't I see it at other times, that
> it is you I love in the beauty of the world and in all the lovely
> girls and dear good friends, and it is pilgrims we are, wayfarers
> on a journey, and not pigs, nor angels.*

When we read the prologue of St. John's Gospel in the light of the Book of Genesis, we see that St. John "fits" the person and significance of Jesus the Christ into the schema of creation and salvation. The prologue echoes Genesis but understands Christ to be the creative word by which God calls creation into existence. The climactic verse in this prologue (v. 14) then asserts: "And the Word became flesh and dwelt among us . . ." That affirmation of John has had so much meaning for the Catholic tradition that when those words were sung at the liturgy the congregation would kneel down at their utterance.**

The point to be emphasized here is that into this God made creation Jesus came and lived. The theological doctrine of creation, in Catholic thought, does not stop with the assertion that God made the world. It adds that the person who is at the center of Christian faith did not dwell in the heavens or "once upon a time." Jesus lived as a real person in a precise moment of human history as one of us in all things save sin. Creation, then, is not merely good but an integral part of the whole plan of God's gracious dealings with his people.

We can now make a generalization which will stand as one basic part of our understanding of the Catholic worldview: our religious faith takes its stand *in this world* and *in human history*. Catholicism should not be conceived as an escape from the world or as a shield from the realities of human events. It is a way of seeing the world, a manner of living in the world, and a strategy for engaging human events. Positively, it means that the world is neither opaque or meaningless; on the contrary, the world is affirmed as good, charged with the presence of God, and, in the words of the psalmist, "tells of the glory of God" (Ps 19:11). In a similar manner, humanity is not an antheap of undifferentiated individuals toiling

---

*Walker Percy, *Love in the Ruins* (New York: Dell Paperback, 1972), p. 104.
**A liturgical usage still customary at the Christmas liturgy.

compulsively and aimlessly until they drop but the crown of God's creation, made in the divine image and likeness, who share their humanity with the Son of God who is the Word made flesh. It is that basic conviction which should be at the root of every attempt to affirm human dignity, to erase anything that degrades people, and to build a better and more beautiful world.

The world and its history is meaning-full not meaning-less, grace-full and not grace-less.

Sin in the World

The above paragraphs about the goodness of the world as gift from the hands of a loving God might well seem preciously pollyannish to those who read the daily papers or watch television with some regularity. What, even a friendly critic might object, has all this talk about the goodness of the created order got to do with the malice, stupidity, greed, and horror of human affairs (to say nothing of the natural disasters) which afflict the world? How does one relate those palpable events which we see every day with this fine, but rather abstract, notion of a good world redeemed by Christ? That question was once posed in the form of a stark statement. At the thought of a tortured and abused child Ivan Karamazov must challenge the right of God to be in contact with humans: "It isn't that I reject God; I am simply returning him most respectfully the ticket that would entitle me to a seat."*

The point is well taken; it has been posed in one form or another since the time of Job who cried out to God asking why there should be such suffering and disappointment in the world of men and women. The answer to those compelling cries—indeed, it is not an answer but an approach to a mystery—is the other side of the Catholic worldview which sees the created world as imperfect and the human condition as one which is prone to evil. The other side of the Catholic worldview, in short, must take account of the fact of sin.

If there is a word which is more misused or time-worn than "sin," I cannot think of it. It is used either in a frivolous manner (calling, for example, a perfume "My Sin") or in such a screeching fashion by popular preachers that it becomes a cliché. Like many

---

*Fydor Dostoevsky, *The Brothers Karamazov* (New York: Bantam, 1970), p. 296.

theological terms it has become so familiar that it resonates with most people like a parody. The problem is exacerbated by the popular linkage of sin and sexuality in our common culture: when someone refers to a "sinful woman" they do not ordinarily have passing bad checks in mind. Even in the common culture of the Church there is a tendency to think of sinning as a breaking of a rule: God sets us some rules and we either obey (and are "good") or we break the rules and are bad—sinners.

We might begin our discussion by making a distinction between sin as a mode of being and sin as a discrete and willful act. At this juncture we are more concerned with sin as a part of the condition of being human.

It is part of Catholic tradition to say that every person born into this world has a propensity toward evil that pushes a person toward acts of autonomy in such a way that they move away from God. The tension between the desire for complete personal autonomy and an acknowledgement of one's dependence on God is one way of looking at the "sinful" state of our human existence. The central message of the basic story of human alienation from God—the story of Adam and Eve in the Book of Genesis—is that our archetypal first parents (our common ancestors) wanted to be "like God" (Gen 3:5). That story is not dissimilar to the description of the fall of Lucifer (the "light bearer") who would not serve God.

That desire for absolute autonomy, that impulse to do and be what we want irrespective of others and the Other, is called, simply, original sin. By affirming the fact that all of us bear within us the sin which is called original the Catholic tradition wishes to affirm two truths: (a) none of us are intrinsically good and (b) none of us are intrinsically corrupt. We are flawed creatures capable of the worst but equally capable of being healed and elevated.

The Catholic doctrine of original sin is an attempt to articulate the reason why we all have impulses to evil and to account for those impulses, often moved to action, in the history of human affairs. The fact of that evil is so clear that it provoked a famous observation by one of the Church's premier thinkers:

And so I argue about the world—if there be a God, *since* there is a God, the human race is implicated in some terrible aboriginal calamity. It is out of joint with the purposes of the creator. This is a fact, a fact as true as the fact of its existence; and thus the doctrine of what is called theologically original sin becomes to me almost as certain as that the world exists, and as the existence of God.*

The sinful *state* of humanity is the matrix out of which arises all the sinful *deeds* that are done by individuals. The tortured child that so worried Ivan Karamazov is tortured by someone, and that someone is impelled by dark and hidden impulses that lead from the good and toward the bad. Moral evil is both the condition of humanity and the ineluctable fact of all human existence. We all know personally its impulses and its hold on us.

The doctrine of original sin could lead, one might object, to either a kind of fatalism ("What's the use? I'm bad by nature") or a profound pessimism about the nature of humanity. Doctrines do not exist in isolation. The notion of original sin must be balanced by the Christian insistence that this sinful state has been healed by the redemptive work of Christ. The condensed symbol of that healing is that which is most identified with Christianity: the cross. It is curious that an instrument of torture, suffering, and death should be used symbolically to say that pain and death are not definitive realities, that they have been overcome. Against any temptation to pessimism because of sin there is the counter-sign of hope which is the cross. That is why St. Paul, in a famous comparison (cf. Rom 5), contrasts the first Adam who brought sin into the world with the second Adam (Christ) who brings deliverance. Paul concludes: "We know that our old self was crucified with him, so that the sinful body might be destroyed and we might no longer be enslaved by sin" (Rom 6:6).

We should add another note. The doctrine of original sin (which includes both the idea of the state of sinfulness and the penchant for sinning) seems implausible or even shocking until we look closely at our own lives and our own moral development as human beings. We all experience a felt gap between what we are and what we ideally should be. We all sense a certain weakness of will when it comes to doing (or avoiding) those things which made us a better person. We all carry our private—and not so private—burdens of shame, disap-

---

*John Henry Newman, *Apologia Pro Vita Sua* (New York: Norton Critical Editions, 1968), p. 187.

pointment, and guilt about our acts and lack of acts. We all know—
even when we are reluctant to openly face the fact—the time when
we have hurt, ignored, abused, or misused other persons and other
things. We all suffer—as everyone from therapists to philosophers
notes—a kind of dis-ease and dis-comfort in our lives. Those "signals
of imperfection" cry out for healing and alleviation.

We also know that some people, allowed free rein for their dis-
ordered impulses, can turn into monsters of depravity as they affirm
their absolute autonomy at the expense of others who are destroyed by
their massive egomania; it happens with a Hitler and it happens, in microcosm, in every neighborhood. None of us is sure that the goodness
overbalances the evil; what we do is hope that the scales can be righted
and fight towards that aim.

That sense of human alienation is not peculiar to individuals; it
manifests itself in human institutions of every social stripe. All our
institutions—churches, corporations, governments—fall short of
stated goals; they have within them a kind of inertia which tugs away
from the good that they set out as their end. Individual levels of
alienation infect social structures since, as the Second Vatican Council says of the consequences of original sin, people fall into "mul-
tiple errors concerning the true God, the nature of man, and the
principles of the moral law. The result has been the corruption of
morals and human institutions and not rarely contempt for the human
person himself.*

At this point, then, we can make a second large generalization
about the Catholic worldview that provides a counterpoint to the first
one: the Catholic tradition rejects the notion that people are intrinsically
good (even if they have a natural dignity in that they are creatures of
God) with their "badness" reducible to accidents of luck, genetics, en-
vironments, or other external factors. People have a propensity toward
evil (exacerbated, to be sure, by external factors) but that propensity is
not so compelling that they escape personal responsibility. On the positive side of this coin, the Catholic tradition proposes the person of Jesus
Christ as the healer of human alienation and as the remedy for what our
tradition calls original sin.

The Catholic worldview is such that, on hearing a report of evil or
wrong-doing, the Catholic should not be surprised that a person was

---

*Decree on the Apostolate of the Laity, II.7, in Documents, p. 497.

capable of doing such a thing; nor should the Catholic be resigned to the fact of evil. The Catholic should be saddened that the old Adam still lives but be convinced absolutely that such moral outrages are not inevitable.

To sum up: The Catholic worldview is not fatalistic or utopian. The Catholic worldview is rooted in a hope-filled realism.

Christian Realism

At the end of the above section we used the term *realism* and it is to that term which we can now turn to set out a third component of our worldview. For our purposes realism will stand for that mediating position which takes into account both the goodness of creation which comes as a gift from God and the fact of human unhappiness and alienation and the sense of incompleteness and imperfection which we call original sin. Christian realism attempts to balance those two doctrines in such a way that there is a coherence and structure to them.*

What does this mean in the concrete?

In the first place it means that the Catholic cannot tolerate a flight from the world in which we live nor accept the notion that this world is all there is. To borrow Walker Percy's formulation: we are neither angels nor pigs. It is good and proper to be sensualists, dreamers, players, thinkers, doers, and lovers. We should live and enjoy the world in which we live. Catholicism is at its best when it is most openly world affirming, sacramental, iconic, and earthy. After all, we are called upon to celebrate the mystery of God through the tactile realities of salt, water, oil, bread, wine, art, and so on. To fully understand Catholicism is to view the word realistically not as angels or beasts but as physical and spiritual human beings.

Second, to recapitulate an earlier point, the Catholic worldview neither accepts the natural perfection of man nor affirms his total depravity. It affirms that we are made "in the image and likeness of God" but it also accepts that we have fallen short of what we ought to be. If realism is a middle position, then we should say that Catholic realism is not starry-eyed about the goodness of people but does not expect the

---

*I am strongly indebted to, but make use of a different sense of, "Christian realism" as it is described by Bernard Lonergan. See Bernard Lonergan, "The Origins of Christian Realism," in *A Second Collection*, ed. Ryan and Terrell (Philadelphia: Westminster, 1974), pp. 239–61.

worst from them either. It is crucial for a sense of Catholic realism that we can look at the most abject of people and see the image of Christ in that person.

The Catholic Church, as a consequence, does not, and has never, viewed itself as a perfectionist sect admitting only the spiritual elite. It has seen itself as a sinful but hope and faith filled people on pilgrimage. The appropriate parabolic description of the Church is the field in which there are both wheat and tares (Mt 13:24ff) with the judgment of Christ alone responsible for the final disposition of both.

One consequence of such a vision of the existence of good and evil has been the traditional Catholic resistance to utopian visions and schemes. Catholic realism does not permit us to find perfection in this life either on an individual or on a social level. Catholicism provides many paths for the seeking of perfection (monasticism, after all, is a kind of utopian fantasy held in check by Christian realism) but it argues that we must stay close to the gritty realities of history and human limitation. People are not good enough to live without government but governments can never provide the all-encompassing framework that gives total meaning to life.

Historically the most persistent temptation of the Catholic tradition has been to lose confidence in the goodness of God's creation. There is an underside to Catholicism largely inherited from the Hellenistic world of neo-Platonism which has denigrated the flesh in the name of a higher and purer life of the spirit. That gnostic spiritualizing temptation has shown itself in a tradition of unhealthy asceticism, a desire for self punishment, and an obsession with the tug of the flesh especially in its sexual manifestation. A fair amount of traditional spirituality and asceticism was tainted—in varying degrees—with a profoundly pessimistic spirit of negative asceticism. That is not to say that asceticism is bad; it is hardly that. What is bad is the attitude that there is something unworthy or evil about the world in which we live and that a sense of its beauty and sensuality is somehow incompatible with living a truly religious life.

The other side of Christian realism is to recognize that there is evil, ugliness, and sin in the world. Yet the evil we confront and the sin we commit is no warrant for fatalism or despair. Catholic realism demands that we affirm that the world itself and *our* world and our life has significance and purpose. It may well be that we are burdened with anxieties or crushing problems of body or spirit that are very real. The

Catholic must try to find the courage to say that these burdens and crosses are not capricious and random events in the universe. Every burden has its meaning and its possibility of being lightened.

In the final analysis we can say that Catholic realism is an attempt to balance our involvement in the real and tactile world with a sense that there is something both beneath and beyond that world; that beneath and beyond is the presence of God.

What Catholic realism says about the world can be applied, with appropriate nuances, to the Catholic view of Jesus. Catholic orthodoxy has always tried to mediate between a picture of Jesus as a divine figure who seemed human and a human who has, as the cliché would have it, a "spark of the divine" in him. Catholic orthodoxy—Catholic realism, if you will—insists that Jesus was a man, a human being and brother who ate, drank, walked, wept, felt, and reacted like other men. He was born of a woman and born into a particular place and time (cf. Gal 4:4). Yet, in Jesus, we do not see only a man albeit a paradigmatic one. In Jesus, we see what God is like. We do not enhance our understanding of the mystery of Jesus by denigrating his humanity or ignoring his divinity. It is in the balance of who he was on earth and what was before, beneath, and beyond that "what he was" that we get the best insight into the nature of the man who was truly God's Son.

By keeping that image of Jesus firmly in mind we can also get a better sense of what it means to be a human being as the Catholic tradition understands being human. If Christ, as St. Paul insists, is the "firstborn of all humanity," then we must say that every human being (i.e. the entire human family of the Second Adam) has another dimension beyond that grasped by human experience or described by human science. To be human, the Catholic tradition insists, is somehow to participate in the divine. That participation is open to all as a birthright. To reject it is, as we have insisted, what sin really is. Catholic realism would remind us that humanity—and that means all of us—are called back to God, but being called means that we must respond.

A final point here: Because we, as Catholics, affirm the goodness of the created order while, simultaneously, admitting the reality of sin, it follows that we must take responsibility for the care of this world entrusted to us and bring it to that perfection which is its end. Some Catholics may be called to go aside to pray and witness to the deeply spiritual values of withdrawal, silence, and solitude, but most of us must live in the world with its intricate network of social relationships—a network which binds us to family, neighborhood, city, state, nation, and world. Catholic realism demands not only that we live in that society but that we contribute to its perfection and its edification (i.e. its "building up"). What that means, in a practical order, is that as Catholics we cannot be passive spectators at the edges of life. To build, to purify, and to add to the family, the commonweal, and human society itself is not just to be a good citizen; it is to be a co-creator with the Creator who not only has given us the world but who holds it in existence with love and concern. Creation is a gift and the arena of the working out of the Christian mystery.

The Experience of Time

There is one final aspect of the Catholic worldview that we need to discuss briefly here although we will return to it later from another perspective. Catholicism is a religion which takes the notion of time very seriously. Christianity does not begin its story "once upon a time." Its temporal indicators speak of the "fullness of time" and the birth of Christ is not given as in the mists of legend but in the time when a "decree went out from Caesar Augustus" (cf. Lk 2:1). Christianity begins in a moment of history and in a definite place. Christ entered our world at a moment in history and the Christian community which witnesses to Christ calls to mind historical moments. Christianity also insists that time is moving toward a final fulfillment.

Catholics perceive time in a threefold manner. It looks to the past for its beginning moments, it celebrates the present as an acceptable time to proclaim the living reality of Jesus, and it looks forward to that which will come in the end time when Jesus returns again. This triple sense of time can be summed up in the economic phrase of St. Augustine of Hippo:

> The present time of past things is memory; the present time of present things is perception; the present time of future things is expectation.*

It is about the past and present that we wish to emphasize here.

The Catholic worldview must embrace the past in a present fashion. What the believing community has learned of Christ and his fol-

---

*The Confessions of St. Augustine, XI.20.

lowing is part of a rich patronage which is preserved, not as a mere memory, but as a living source which enriches us today. As Catholics we constantly look back to our writers, our saints, our traditions, our art, and our teachers to help us see how we should live today. We inquire of a St. Francis how we should love the poor; we look to a St. Thomas or a St. Augustine to ask how we should think about our faith; we inquire of St. Teresa of Avila about the life of prayer; we look to our history to learn of both failure and success; we search our art and liturgy for appropriate models of edification; we remember our missionaries to help us nourish zeal. Everything that the Church does is saturated in the memory of the community of faith which has gone before us. Our catholicity is not just the catholicity of the moment but also the catholicity of memory.

To remember a tradition only because it is a tradition is the task of the antiquarian. We remember our tradition in the present for two reasons: (a) to express solidarity and fellowship with "those who have gone to their rest in the hope of rising again"* since they are also part of the community of praise, and (b) to express our conviction that we are the heirs of the New Testament Church. To put it another way: We look at our community of faith as an organic one growing in space and time. The Church is not a mere social reality existing in the here and now. We are the present sign and presence of a community which has a vibrant reality in the unfolding of human history.

When we gather for the liturgy on Sunday we consciously and explicitly link our present worship with the past. Indeed, one could say that the pre-eminent act of celebrating the past in the present is the celebration of the Eucharist which is a re-presenting of Christ among us. We should also note, in line with what we have mentioned earlier, that this re-presentation also gives us hope for the future. The liturgy is a celebration of memory, presence, and expectation:

> When we eat this bread and drink this cup, we proclaim your death,
> Lord Jesus, until you come in glory.**

In those affirmations we affirm, then, past, present, and future. Our present experience must make reference to the "not yet" of

---

Eucharistic Prayer II.
**Eucharistic Proclamation.*

Christ's promises. That expectation must not be construed as a passive "waiting around" for the coming of the Lord. Expectation in the Catholic tradition is linked to the notion that the future is built by those who cooperate in making the presence of Christ a present reality in this world. We accept in faith that somehow—as with a mustard seed—Christ's kingdom is already here in an inchoate and yet unrealized form. Our task is to deepen, extend, and perfect that kingdom until the day of the Lord when "it will be brought into full flower."*

A Summary Statement

We can encapsulate the basic thrust of this chapter briefly: A Catholic Christian is a member of a living and visible community which constantly recalls that the world and its history, as imperfect and sinful as it might appear, is a gift and a sign from God which has been entrusted to us to cultivate. Being a Catholic, then, does not mean to be (or to do) apart from the basic task of living as fully conscious and responsible human beings with both individual and social destinies. To the degree that one lives as fully as possible in Christ, both as individuals and as members of society, we extend the kingdom which Christ has already announced and which we re-present when "two or three are gathered" in the name of Jesus.

To look out at the world in a Catholic fashion is to reject two polar attitudes which the Catholic Church always resists. One attitude would insist that this material world is all there is; the most vulgar form of Marxism is the definitive assertion that materialism is at the root and heart of human life. The Catholic worldview would resist that understanding of reality by saying that beneath, beyond, in front of, and behind this world is a horizon of mystery which is good, purposeful, caring, and accessible. It would further insist that the way to touch that mystery is to know Jesus the Christ who is the revelation of the mystery to us in this historical order.

The other attitude which the Church rejects is that which would affirm a reality beyond this world in such a way that denigrates the world or sees it as evil, opaque, and an obstacle to knowing the divine.

_he Pastoral Constitution on the Church in the Modern World, III.39. It is remarkable how much the epoch-making document of the Second Vatican Council insists on the task of building t..e world while waiting for the Lord to come in glory.

We cannot insist too much that the central affirmation of Christianity—that the Word became flesh; that God became man—is the surest and most persistent antidote to that notion. In the incarnation we have the irreducible affirmation that our world, given as a gift, is enhanced and dignified by the entry of the Son of God into the grittiness and reality of human life and human history.

It is from this basis of realism that the Church ultimately affirms a good deal of what is fundamental to it: the incarnation and the entire notion of sacramentality and mediation. It is precisely because we can have confidence in the world that we can also affirm that God dwells among us and that the visible signs of the world and the Church can mediate the mysteries of God to us. This attitude also underpins the desire of the Church to heal the wounded, aid the downtrodden, set forth images of hope to the despairing, demand that justice roll down like waters, and so forth. It is often said by the cynical that Church people are "do-gooders"—but that "do-gooding" has a basis in the very way the Church sees the world and its mission in it.

Christian realism also demands that we accept the judgment that the Church as a community often fails in its mission. We must affirm again—it is the message of Christian realism—that the community of believers which is the Church is hardly exempt from the passions and sins of the world. To the degree that the Church can overcome its lassitude and weakness to be faithful to Christ, it *becomes* more Catholic since "Catholic" is not a description of what is but what should be.

It does not take a great deal of research to discover that what the Church does (or strives to do) seems a mystery and even a scandal to the world. Catholic realism could predict that; Catholic hope, despite the indifference of the world, still calls us to reaffirm our vision and to proclaim the truth of God. Indeed, that seems to be the crucial mission of the Church when it is viewed in relationship to the world. That task of the Church has been very well summed up by one of our most distinguished contemporary theologians, the Dutch Dominican, Edward Schillebeeckx:

> . . . there is an indissoluble bond between religion and the world. God cannot be reached outside his own manifestations and he never coincides with any of them. Thus, there is a necessary conjunction between appearance and obscurement. That is why it is possible to forget God and be silent about him. Now religions and the church

are precisely the *anamnesis,* the memory of this universal salvific will and saving presence of God, ground of all hope. The churches keep that universal saving presence from lapsing into oblivion, thanks to their religious word and sacrament.*

Points for Discussion

(a) The Catholic worldview is rooted in gratitude. Have you ever thought out your own feelings of gratitude for life and all that comes with it? In what ways can you cultivate that "mystical minimum of gratitude" which is basic to our reaction to the world and to life itself?

(b) While we might not call ourselves "sinners," we ought to be aware of that deep-rooted attitude (orientation) which keeps us from being more open, loving, and generous. To what extent do you realize that about yourself?

(c) Do you have a sense of responsibility for the building up of our world and our culture? How can you foster a sense of the world as a gift entrusted to us for cultivation?

(d) Do you have a keen sense of the passage of time, our responsibility in time, and our instinct to celebrate times in our lives?

(e) Could you set out a Catholic "credo" that would encompass a basic Catholic worldview?

---

*Robert J. Schreiter, ed., *The Schillebeeckx Reader* (New York: Crossroad, 1984), p. 257.

Chapter VIII

Spirituality

If we accept Cicero's notion that the word *religion* literally means "to bind" (Lat. *religare*) or connect us with God, then we can say that Catholicism's essence is not to be found in its long history, noble traditions, good works, or involvement in the great issues of human ethics but in its capacity to keep us close to—bound to—God. More specifically, since Catholicism confesses Jesus as Lord, Catholicism only makes sense in terms of its witness to the living reality of Jesus the Christ and the resources it possesses to make God in Christ real and palpable to those in the Church and as a possibility for those whom the Church witnesses to outside its community.

At a certain level this is all obvious. Almost everything the Church does and is in a visible observable manner—from buildings to books— is connected in some way to making manifest Christ, however badly or clumsily done those attempts might sometimes seem to be. Yet, in another sense, the manifestation of Christ can be a difficult and slippery enterprise. The Church, seen as a visible reality, can be as hostile a place for the presence of Christ as the most "secular" of institutions. We all know that from sad experience. In my parish (or family or neighborhood or religious order or . . .) we know people who identify themselves as Catholics (we may be numbered among them) in an open or even aggressive manner but who seem to be totally untouched with what are the most basic values of the Gospel. In fact, we often find people in the Church who are bitter, cynical, indifferent, or even despairing. They are in the Church but the Church seems not to touch them in its essentials. The point is this: being in the Church is no *de facto* guarantee of growth in Christ; being in the Church only offers proximity to those resources by which we can grow in Christ.

One of the commonest words in the Catholic vocabulary is *grace*. At its most fundamental level grace is the self-giving of God as a purely free gesture. In that sense creation is a grace as is every other gesture of God toward us. The supreme grace, of course, is Jesus himself. Since grace is a gift it can, like every gift, be rejected, received without gratitude, mishandled, or treasured. Every grace implies both a giver and a recipient. If we think of God in Christ constantly oriented toward us, we can say that being recipients of God's grace means nothing else than our recognition of God's self-giving and our acceptance of that gift. Grace, in short, is the gracious acceptance of God; it is saying "yes" to the gift.

How do we utter that "yes" to God? That acceptance occurs in many diverse ways ranging from a dramatic acceptance of a conversion experience (e.g. the road to Damascus conversion of Paul) to those small utterances of "yes" by which we start again in the face of our petty derelictions and acts of omission. For the vast majority of us our conversions are not overwhelming once-in-a-lifetime moments. Most of us find that the process of conversion is just that: a conversion. If we respond to God's call with a "yes" we find that our growth in faith is a series of incremental steps by which we reach toward new insights and/or modes of action by which we apply the Gospel to the living out of our lives. Those conversionary steps of growth may come as easily as the fact of maturing or growing up itself or they may result from the pains, disappointments, or tragedies which drive us to a more acute sense of enveloping need in our lives.

That process of learning to say "yes" to God is called spirituality. The word *spirituality* is a relatively new one in the Catholic vocabulary. As late as the seventeenth century it had a rather pejorative ring to it and meant something that was precious or even gnostic in piety. Even today it has such a certain elitist ring that a contemporary Orthodox theologian, Alexander Schmemann, has suggested that we simply substitute the word "Christian life," for it is that which the word "spirituality" is meant to convey today.* We shall use the term spirituality since it is so common, but we shall understand it in Professor Schmemann's sense of the word. Spirituality will simply mean in this chapter that complex of beliefs, attitudes, and practices by which the presence of Christ is made more manifest in the lives of believers and by which we are led more fully and openly to say "yes" to the gift of God.

Prayer

There is a popular tendency to think of prayer as the recitation of formulas (i.e. "saying" prayers) or direct monologues to God. A

---

*See "Spirituality," in *The Westminster Dictionary of Christian Spirituality*, ed. G. S. Wakefield (Philadelphia: Westminster, 1984), pp. 360ff.

wit once said that "speaking to God is prayer; God speaking to us is called schizophrenia." We shall begin with the old penny cate-chism definition that prayer is the "lifting of the heart and mind to God." However familiar that definition is, it is still an excellent one because it says, implicitly, that prayer, before all else, is a gesture of attention directed away from the self and toward that other whom we call God. That verb "lifting" signifies a turn away from the daily round of our existence toward that reality which is God. In the broadest possible sense, then, prayer is an *attitude* by which we take into account the reality of God in our lives. When we grasp that prayer is an attitude, we can then go on to explore the ways in which that attitude or situation is expressed in our lives. In fact, there are so many facets and examples of prayer in the memory of Catholicism that we can easily think that it is not one thing but many. The point we wish to emphasize is the opposite: prayer is a gestural attitude of expressing the reality of God, and that basic gestural attitude takes many forms.

Liturgical Prayer. Liturgical prayer means those activities which are connected to the public official worship of the Church: the solemn office of monastic and religious praise which is called the Divine Office and those public sacramental and liturgical acts of worship of the Church. Most of us experience the liturgical prayer of the Church most frequently in our participation at Sunday wor-ship. In those solemn acts and gestures the Church gathers as a pub-lic community and expresses the most common forms of prayer: the act of adoration, the act of thanksgiving, the act of begging for-giveness, and petitions for needs both spiritual and temporal.

Behind all of those forms of prayer in the liturgy, however, is the fundamental act of acknowledgement. By our very act of worship we say, in effect, that we are not totally autonomous, self-sufficient or self-explanatory, self-contained beings. We acknowledge, posi-tively, a state of being contingent on God. We need to emphasize a point here that we have made previously in this volume: when we go to church to participate in the liturgy by hearing the word and celebrating the mysteries of the Eucharist we are making, in the first instance, an act of worship and expressing an act of faith. No matter how routine those gestures may be and no matter how accustomed we are to making them, they do say, at the very least, that we pub-licly acknowledge something else in life.

To say "yes" to God in liturgical prayer means that we go beyond the gestures that are automatic in order to fully and consciously affirm what the gestures mean and signify. It is only when we begin to act as conscious *human* participants in the liturgy that the words and gestures can have a shaping influence on our lives. It is good to go to Mass; it is better to go and to listen and respond and share and participate. It is even better to allow the words and gestures to shape the consciousness so that a fuller Christian life begins to emerge. An adult may have heard and recited the Lord's Prayer thousands of times at Sunday Mass as a formal act but only rarely listened to the words or tried to assimilate them into one's consciousness and way of acting. The point is that the liturgy, in all of its manifestations, admits of many levels of entry ranging from the purely formalistic to the deepest and most contemplative. One penetrates to the heart of liturgical prayer only to the extent that one converts to what the liturgy means to convey; that process is a lifelong turning to the self-gift of God in worship.

Students often tell me in my office that they do not go to church (people have a compulsion to tell their religious stories to theology professors) because they "get nothing out of it." My invariable response to that statement, however much I may understand it, is that they have it backward. The first obligation of Catholics is to give—not get—something (even if the giving is nothing more than their presence) before they can expect something in return. The life of public prayer must begin with those formal gestures by which we explicitly acknowledge the fact of God in our lives.

Private Prayer. By private prayer I mean not only those private personal moments of prayer or saying prayers but also those social occasions (like prayers before meals or other family prayers) which are not part of the official prayer life of the liturgy of the Church. Here again the formulas of prayer (e.g. the recitation of this prayer or that one before retiring for the evening) is less central than the gesture itself. The simple act of saying grace before meals—however little we may advert to the words or the act itself—is a gesture of gratitude which can be nourished by a cultivation of reflection. The very act of saying grace is a gesture of thanksgiving, and its omission would be a diminution of the spirit of gratitude toward God.

Private prayer is, of course, more than a simple impersonal gesture. Prayer is a making visible and real our needs, aspirations, and dispositions. The wide range of Catholic devotional practices ranging from such traditional acts as saying the rosary or making the stations of the cross to the recitations of favorite prayers or exuberantly "praying in the Spirit" among charismatic Catholics testifies not only to the long history of the Church with its care to conserve worthwhile devotional practices but also to the varying needs and tastes of people in the ways in which they express their devotion. In one small but visible way, the plethora of devotional modes is a sign of the Church's catholicity. In its spiritual repertoire there are prayer forms to attract and, to be honest, offend almost everyone. The prayer life of the Church may fulfill the desire for emotional exuberance, austerity, colorful detail, or considered detachment. Indeed, many people have observed over the years that one could do a sociological profile of human spiritual needs and "tastes" by the simple process of studying the varying forms of the Catholic prayer life. It is an area not much studied by theologians, but it increasingly gets attention as scholars begin to pay attention to what is often called—a bit patronizingly—"popular" religion.

Prayer as Discipline. From its very beginnings the Catholic tradition has had a place for those who wished to pursue the life of prayer with enough intensity and regularity to make the experience of God a felt reality and the center of existence. From the experiences of the desert fathers and mothers in the third century through the rise of monastic life in the early Middle Ages to the great flowerings of mysticism in thirteenth century Italy and fourteenth century Germany, and through the post-Reformation period, there has been a constant witness in the Church to a life which is completely given over to prayer and contemplation. This tradition, like that of the tradition of popular devotion, has had many and varied forms. It allows for the silence and solitude of the Carthusian hermit, the austere contemplation of the Carmelite nun, the passionate Christ mysticism of the Franciscan, and the rigorous intellectuality of the Ignatian tradition or combinations of all of these. The various methods, traditions, schools, and doctrines of prayer and contemplation are too numerous even to list in this book. We can indicate the generalized lines that give shape to all of them in a basic fashion. There are, in short, certain constants that can be detected.

First, there is an insistence that silence, both external (a silent place) and internal (the quieting of the heart and mind), is a prerequisite to genuine prayer. It is not simply a question of removing exterior noise but a disciplined willingness to shut off the distractions of the environment, even "good" distractions, in order to listen to the promptings of God in the heart. Silence, in the tradition of prayer, means nothing more than alertness or readiness to receive God; it is another form of saying "yes" to the promptings of God's self-gift.

Second, all of the spiritual masters and mistresses agree that while prayer may begin with forms of prayer and formal gestures (reading meditatively, reciting prayers with attention, "thinking about God" in a discursive manner, etc.), there will come a time, if one is faithful, when words/gestures will fall off and the prayerful person enters a state of simple presence and quiet before the mystery of God. One is in the presence, not of an object, but of the Other who is source, love, and full meaning of life. Paradoxically enough, when one begins to experience that kind of prayer there is an alternation of happiness and consolation mingled with periods of doubts and fears—some so intense that St. John of the Cross, one of the greatest mystics, has called such periods the "dark night" of the soul. To pray at this level of simplicity requires great faith and openness to God. The experience of simple prayer has been beautifully described by one of the great spiritual masters of our time, the monk and writer, Thomas Merton:

> I have a very simple way of prayer. It is centered entirely on attention to the presence of God and to His will and love. That is to say that it is centered on faith by which we alone can know the presence of God. . . . Yet it does not mean imagining anything or conceiving a precise image of God, for to my mind that would be a kind of idolatry. On the contrary, it is a matter of adoring Him as invisible and infinitely beyond our comprehension and realizing Him as all. There is in my heart this great thirst to recognize totally the nothingness of all that is not God.*

Finally, all of the great persons of prayer tell us that the experience of prayer should make a profound difference and a deep change in our life. The dim experiential sense of God in prayer ought

---

*The Hidden Ground of Love: The Letters of Thomas Merton, edited by William H. Shannon (New York: Farrar, Straus, and Giroux, 1985), pp. 63–64.

to transform a person, make him or her more compassionate and open, more of a vessel of the Gospel, more of a sign to other people. That is why, historically, people have sought out spiritual masters and mistresses for their aid and comfort. That is why the greatest "activist" saints, whether in the intellectual life (e.g. Thomas Aquinas) or in the life of charity (Vincent de Paul) or in the prophetic ministry (Catherine of Siena), have also been acknowledged virtuosos of prayer. Their words and deeds rise up from, but remain rooted in, deep and felt awareness of God known face to face. That is why the popular story tradition of the Church is filled with stories of persons of "low" stations—doorkeepers at convents, wanderers, farm help, etc.—who have been sought out as counselors or feared as prophetic voices who chide the wealthy or the learned. The tradition of the person who is a *Christus absconditus* (a "hidden Christ") is a cautionary and an exemplary tale, for it tells us that the most authentic voices in the life of the Church are those who do not excel necessarily in learning and dignity but who have tasted deeply of the experience of God.

Models

One of the characteristic features of the Catholic tradition is its veneration of the saints. The fact that we ask the saints (in the liturgy, for example) to intercede for us before God is simply a way of affirming that the Catholic Church feels a bond not only with the Church on earth as it exists in the here and now but also with those who already enjoy God's presence in heaven. That bond between the Church here on earth and those who "sleep the sleep of peace" is called the communion of saints.

The saints are also remembered in the tradition of the Church because through their remembered lives they help remind us of the diversity of ways that can be lived out in the following of Christ. We point out certain extraordinary persons who have lived before us whose lives are instructive in the insights they manifest in the living out of the Gospels. Such persons, in the formulation of the theologian David Tracy, are "classics"—they both sum up and then advance our understanding of the Gospel as a lived reality.* Thus, for

---

*David Tracy, *The Analogical Imagination* (New York: Crossroad, 1981); see also Lawrence S. Cunningham, *The Meaning of Saints* (San Francisco: Harper and Row, 1980).

example, we cannot discuss the meaning of evangelical poverty in the contemporary world without taking into account the way St. Francis of Assisi lived out a life of poverty in the Middle Ages. We cannot begin to think about the life of prayer without reference to the great masters and mistresses of prayer (Teresa of Avila, John of the Cross, Julian of Norwich, etc.) who have gone before us. What the great saints do is to point out, with their very lives, new possibilities and new ways of the *imitatio Christi*. The great saints also show us that the life of the Gospel is still a possibility. In our time the world has been enchanted with Mother Teresa of Calcutta. When one considers her work and life it is clear that she is doing what the great saints have been doing for millennia: serving the most destitute of society out of love for Christ. If one were to transport her back a thousand years her work would be the same. What her life teaches is that the essentials of the Gospel never change. She serves as a visible sign of the continued vitality and attractiveness of the message and person of Jesus. A person like Mother Teresa also serves as a counter-sign to the flaccid commitments we all make to the Gospel by showing that one must risk and spend all in the service of God.

One cannot speak of Christian models in the Catholic tradition without reference to Mary, the Mother of Jesus. Mary is a central figure in Catholic piety and Catholic theology. Theologically, Mary, described as the Mother of God (*Theotokos*), is the historic way in which the Church has attempted to guarantee and strengthen the central doctrine of the incarnation. Mary was the Mother of the person who was both human and divine. Metaphorically Mary is seen as the central *figura* of the Church. Just as Mary brought Christ into the world physically, so the Church brings forth Christ through grace, witness, and the sacraments. It is not an accident that we refer to the Church as a mother: *Sancta Mater Ecclesia:* Holy Mother the Church. Devotionally, Mary is seen as the intercessor between God and the believing community. She is invoked in every liturgy and in almost all Catholic prayers.

The place and role of Mary in the history and development of the Catholic tradition is a fascinating but complex one. While official Catholic theology has always made a sharp distinction between the *adoration* of God and the *veneration* of the Virgin, the popular piety of the various ages perceived Mary as an all-powerful woman who could demand, as she did in the twelfth century, sanctuaries like the great Gothic cathedrals of Chartres, Paris, and Amiens to honor her. The slow development of the cult of Mary in the history of the Catholic tradition allowed for the "feminization" of the divine in a religion which seems unremittingly masculine.

The devotional tradition involving Mary did seem excessive and/or sentimental at times. It was a sticking point with the sixteenth century reformers. It was an ominous sign that in the sixteenth century one saw, more and more, art in which the Virgin was depicted without reference to Christ so that she took on a symbolic existence of her own. There was also a great outburst of Marian speculation of a rather exaggerated and baroque nature. Those tendencies led the Second Vatican Council to reintegrate the place of Mary into a wider theological framework; it is worth noting that the Council resisted the idea of setting out a separate document on Mary. Nonetheless, the Council did affirm (or, better, reaffirm) the legitimacy and desirability of devotion to Mary while, at the same time, insisting that Mary and her place in the life of the Church is only explicable when "related to Christ, the source of all truth, sanctity, and piety."*

In this post-conciliar period we still look to Mary but from the vantage point of our contemporary experience and our own needs. For the poor of the world, especially the poor of Latin America, Mary continues as the protectress of the downtrodden peasant and the urban rootless. Mexicans still honor the Virgin of Guadalupe not only because she is a dark-skinned *mestiza* like themselves but because she is the champion of the poor. Contemporary liberation theologians point to Mary's Magnificat (cf. Lk 1:46–55) with its theme of identification of the poor who hope in God (the *anawim* of the Bible) and their ultimate exaltation when they will be "filled with good things" while the rich "will be sent away hungry." Mary, in this understanding, gives both dignity and hope to the poor. She is not a sign of passive acceptance but a symbol of hope and aspiration which explains why—in the Mexican context—the Virgin of Guadalupe figures so prominently in the iconography of protest and reform.

Recent biblical studies on Mary in the New Testament** has revealed in rich detail how Mary was understood in the earliest theologies of the infant Church. For the Catholic Mary is the perfect Christian,

---

*Dogmatic Constitution on the Church, VIII.4.67, in *Documents*, p. 94.

**See, among others, the fine study of Raymond Brown *et al.*, *Mary in the New Testament* (Philadelphia: Fortress, 1978) written from an ecumenical perspective.

obedient to God's call, a model for the believer, a true disciple, a fellow sufferer in this life, a worthy friend, and a sister for all of humanity. It is for that reason that Sunday after Sunday the liturgy honors the ever Virgin Mary Mother of Jesus Christ "in union with the whole Church." This sense of Mary is profoundly rooted in the Catholic sensibility. It says much of what Catholicism is. In a recent book Andrew Greeley and Mary Durkin write:

> Mary is the litmus paper, the touchstone. She represents the genius of the Catholic sensibility and also the pre-1960 ossification and desiccation of it. She also represents the power of the sensibility to survive the madcap faddism of the post-Vatican council era. The elites may not notice her. They may abhor rosaries and May crown-ings. Yet Mary is alive and well in the Catholic imagination.*

Catholics look, first, to Mary and then to the other saints and he-roes of her tradition to teach us about living the Gospel. We honor the long train of apostles, martyrs, confessors, and the others who make up the honor roll of the tradition. Our admiration extends to those who are canonized (i.e. those whom the Church recognizes as worthy of public veneration in the liturgy, those who are on the list—the canon—of the saints) and those who are not. We consider with wonder the peasant piety and prophetic eye of a Pope like the late John XXIII; the boundless charity of a Teresa of Calcutta or a Dorothy Day; the selfless life of an Oscar Romero; the prayerful depths of a Simone Weil or Thomas Mer-ton. In all of their lives we find a yardstick with which we measure our own fidelity to Christ.

Nowhere is the catholicity of the Church better measured than in its catalogue of the saints. As we browse through the many standard dictionaries of the saints one sees peasants and kings, queens and re-formed prostitutes, hermits and people of the world, monks and married folks, men and women who range from the lovable to the fanatic, the learned and the ignorant, the noble and the humble. In that bewildering procession we find those who are our near contemporaries and others who might exist only in the mists of legend or who are the creation of overheated religious minds. As a whole they are as varied as are all the pilgrims who make up the Church in history. What they all give witness

---

*Andrew M. Greeley and Mary Greeley Durkin, *How To Save the Catholic Church* (New York: Viking, 1984), p. 257.

to, however, is the persistent desire of those who seek out Christ. Some of them are very much creatures of their own time while others, like a St. Francis or a St. Thomas More, so transcend their own time that they become permanent resources for those who are on the spiritual journey.

All of our models do not come from the public rank of the saints. Many of us find our models among those with whom we communicate spiritually and materially on a daily basis. The process of edification (that badly misused word means "to build up") occurs every time we meet for common prayer, every time we diminish our own ego to reach out to another, every time we run across examples of fidelity or love or courage or compassion in the lives of others.

Throughout this book we have insisted—and insist yet again here—that the Church is a community of believers who do more than gather together accidentally or out of a mere common interest.

The Church is at its most vital when its neighbors aid each other to find Christ through worship and action. That communion is what builds up the body of Christ. It is very easy to overlook the powerful forces working on us close to home. We do not have to go to Butler's *Lives of the Saints* to be edified. Do we not all know people in our parish or neighborhood who have suffered and triumphed out of great religious conviction? Do we not always marvel at a family who loves and cares for a mentally handicapped child or an ill parent or a wayward child? Have we not all met a priest or religious who was really extraordinary and to whom we felt free to go to for advice or encouragement? Is it not true that most of us are the Catholic Christians we are today not because of the saints in the canon but through the example of those who in the Church touched us deeply and showed us what it meant to live as a Catholic? Long before most of us read about the great saints, we were in touch with parents, teachers, clerics, and fellow worshipers who taught us with their lives what it means to be a person of faith and prayer. And is this not when it is recognized a dramatic show of that edification of the Church which is the body of Christ?

Sources

We have stated above that we grow in Christ through prayer and with the aid of the example of others. What stands behind prayer? What energizes the saints and heroes of the faith? The simple answer, of course, is Christ. The more complete answer is Christ as he is discovered in the Scriptures and encountered in the sacramental life of the Church. The foundation of all Christian spirituality ultimately rests on a fidelity in hearing God's word and an intimacy with Christ through the reception of the Eucharist. In sum: it is in the liturgy that we find the source and heart of all Catholic spirituality. We started this book with a consideration of the "typical" parish not only because it is one of the easiest ways to observe the life of the Church but also because, most typically, it is there that we find the very heart of Catholic spirituality: it is where the word is authentically preached and the Eucharist is celebrated.*

It is with the above affirmation that a number of themes begin to come together. We insist on the "ordinary" or "typical" experience of the Catholic as he or she attends the liturgy. The claim we make is that in the liturgy—with its word and sacrament—we have the fundamental and indispensable resources for Christian nurture and growth. We hear the word of God in that celebration just as it has been claimed from the beginning of the Christian era. We celebrate the Eucharist, proclaiming in that act that "God is with us."

Again, energized by that encounter in the liturgy, we then go out into the world of the workaday with the command to live out what we have professed. Every other aspect of Catholic spirituality—from contemplative retreat to active missionary life—can be seen as an intensification of that fundamental encounter with Christ in the liturgy.

It may be objected that Catholicism also puts a large emphasis on private prayer, private meditation, and personal spiritual growth through various non-liturgical exercises. Of that fact, there is no doubt. From the early desert fathers and mothers who infrequently participated in the liturgy to the admonitions of *The Imitation of Christ* in the late Middle Ages to stay in one's room in silent meditation, there has been a tradition in the Catholic Church which has put a strong emphasis on self-examination, silent meditation, solitude and so on. What must be remembered, however, is that these activities cannot be viewed as discrete exercises free from (or detached from) the central celebration of the liturgy. They are complementary to this public life of the Church.

---

*This emphasis on the parish must be understood in a non-exclusive manner. People may hear the word and celebrate the Eucharist in college chapels, small groups, mission churches, etc. The parish is my short-hand way of speaking to emphasize the liturgy.

The matter has been succinctly stated by one of the great contemporary masters of the contemplative life:

> The early Christian tradition and the spiritual writers of the middle ages knew no conflict between "public" and "private" prayer, or between the liturgy and contemplation. This is a modern problem. Or perhaps it would be more accurate to say that it is a pseudo-problem. Liturgy by its very nature tends to prolong itself in individual prayer and mental prayer in its turn disposes itself for and seeks fulfillment in liturgical worship.*

Readers at this point may say that they are in agreement about the centrality of the liturgy but object, at the practical level, that the liturgy as they experience it does not, in fact, lead them to a deeper sense of Christ. The specific objection, which we have all heard *ad nauseam,* is that the parish liturgy is slovenly celebrated, the readings are unintelligible, the hymns banal and second rate, the sermons an insult to the intelligence, and the whole ensemble unspeakably dreary. There is just too much that is formulaic about the liturgy. The words drone by without punch and the rites are rather like perfunctory gestures well worn from use but devoid of meaning.

The objection is a serious one and the frequency with which it is heard makes it not a lament but a problem to be faced. What Walker Percy says about the Christian novelist has equal applicability to the state of the ordinary Christian who is trying to *hear* and *speak* the good news:

> The Christian novelist nowadays is like a man who has found a treasure hidden in the attic of an old house, but he is writing for people who have moved out to the suburbs and who are bloody sick of the old house and everything in it.**

What is to be done? Two observations are in order. First, those who preside at liturgy must realize that they have a serious obligation to provide, not stones, but bread. In this age of direct mass communication there is absolutely no excuse for slovenly liturgies and/or poor sermons. There was a time when Catholics were reinforced by a sense

---

*Thomas Merton, *Contemplative Prayer* (New York: Herder, 1969), p. 55.

**Walker Percy, *The Message in the Bottle* (New York: Farrar, Straus, and Giroux), p. 116.

of duty and a feeling of guilt to "attend Mass" no matter how badly celebrated it may have been. That is no longer the case. People today, rightly or wrongly, vote with their feet. They simply will not come to churches where there is nothing but empty formalism. Priests today are called upon to be everything from business managers of their parish "plant" to counselors and therapists for their parishioners' problems and a lot in between. But, *above everything else,* they are celebrants of the liturgy and preachers of the word; if they fail in that, they fail. Period.

Second, the lay person also has a role in this matter. Parishioners should see that the parish is so structured that the priests of the parish can fulfill their responsibilities. Priests are not ordained to raise monies or oversee the repair of the school roof. The parish must be so supported that trivial pursuits do not eat up the time of the priests. At the same time the parishioners and congregates have a right in justice to demand that they get well thought out sermons and decent liturgies. People should fight to sustain that right. One person who complains may be dismissed as a pain in the neck; ten who complain may be a disaffected minority; but when a hundred complain we see a reform movement afoot. There ought to be ways to do this without contentiousness or bitterness, but it ought to be done if the parish is to be a vibrant reality.

Finally, we must reiterate what we have said in an earlier context about the relationship of spirituality and the life of action. That relationship is a dialectical one: the one feeds off the other with both parts of the dialectic crucial if vitality is to be maintained. One of the persistent concerns of our best contemporary spiritual writers is to show that any alleged split between the "active" and "contemplative" life is, in fact, a false split. To over-praise the active life (get out of the monastery and help the poor!) or the contemplative life (the sole aim of life is to cultivate my praise of God) is to run a series of risks that can be destructive of an authentic Christian life. The activist, who is not rooted in a life of prayer and reflection, runs the real risk of burnout; the contemplative with no real sense of care and compassion for the other can easily become self-absorbed and narcissistic. The greatest contemplatives of the Catholic tradition have always insisted that a deep spirituality brings with it a sense of the needs of the Church and the world. St. Thérèse of Lisieux (1873–1897) spent her entire adult life (from the age of fifteen) as a cloistered Carmelite nun in France. She was called to be a woman of silent prayer. Yet she is the patroness of all foreign missionaries not because she went abroad as a missionary but because she expressed her explicit solidarity in prayer with those who did, in fact, go out to evangelize. From the hiddenness of her cloister she reflected the deepest sense of catholicity in that she saw her life, not in an atomized fashion, but as a part of the great enterprise of the entire Church. For Thérèse the needs of the Church and the world were not extraneous to, but firmly linked with, the life of prayer.

We who are "ordinary" Catholics combine the active and contemplative life in less dramatic ways. Ideally, we participate in the worship of the Church in such a fashion that both word and sacrament nourish us. That nourishment sustains us in our life and leads us back again, to the liturgy and the life of prayer, to be nourished yet again. If we are serious about our commitment to the life of prayer and the life of the Church, we consciously attempt to "carry over" what we experience in the liturgy into our mundane life. When, for example, we hear Christ's demand that we forgive proclaimed in the liturgy, we ideally remember that we must forgive in the precincts of the family, the schoolroom, the workplace. When we hear the great prophetic cry for justice and mercy, we do not think that justice is a political matter but a virtue to be exercised in the here and now according to the needs and circumstances of the lived life. There is no need to multiply examples here; the point is a simple one: there needs to be some correlation between what we profess in the liturgy and how we live. We take on the life-long task of "translating" words into deeds and real-life gestures.

The relationship between worship and life has two other refinements which need to be mentioned. First, what we affirm in worship stands as a kind of check and standard that helps us judge the quality and character of our life. By reflection on the liturgical meaning we can, if we are honest, assess the quality and seriousness of our daily life. At that level, then, reflective worship acts in a prophetic manner in our life: it judges us. Seen from another perspective, our life in the daily round of ordinary living should send us back to the liturgy and the life of devotion both as an act of thanksgiving and as an opportunity for petition. Both those levels are part of the larger dialectic of life as worship; that authentic worship is, in the words of the Council, "the primary and indispensable source from which the faithful are to derive the true Christian spirit."*

---

*The Constitution on the Sacred Liturgy, II.14, in Documents, p. 144.

Points for Discussion

(a) Do you have (would you care to have) a disciplined life of prayer?

(b) How best can you integrate the life of liturgical prayer (i.e. going to Mass) with your private devotional life?

(c) Who are your spiritual models? What about these models most attract you to them?

(d) There are different "styles" or "tastes" in the spiritual life. Which do you find most attractive? Repugnant? Why?

(e) Have you thought out any practical strategies to link your own sense of spirituality to your active life as a Christian? Which strategies seem most productive? Problematical?

Chapter IX

Christian Living:
The Moral Life

$\mathbf{T}$here is an unhappy tendency to equate religious life with external forms of behavior. There is a common stereotype which depicts Catholics as following a set of imperatives that make up the framework of their behavior: Catholics *must* go to Mass on Sundays; Catholics *must not* marry before anyone except a priest; Catholics shall do this and they shall not do that. This is a very impoverished view of Catholicism but it is a view that must be blamed, in part, on aspects of the Catholic tradition itself. Over its long history the Catholic Church has evolved a very complex moral code that originated with its meditation on the Scriptures and the rigorous application of philosophical, legal, and social norms to behavior. This process can be described as a kind of moral reasoning. It derives from questions. The Bible forbids, in the ten commandments, killing: "Thou shall not kill." The question that arises is: Is this true for the soldier who fights? for the person defending home and family? for the state when it wishes to execute a felon? Those questions *inevitably* lead to other questions: If it is legitimate for a soldier to kill another combatant in war is it lawful if the rulers over the army are waging an unjust war? Can one kill to defend property? The more questions that are asked, the more answers appear, and more "rules" arise. Catholic moral theory, in other words, evolved the way civil or criminal law evolves: through the application of principles ("Thou shall not kill") to concrete situations (the role of the soldier).

The net result of this long process of moral reasoning was a system in the Church that was quite capable of (a) determining that certain forms of behavior were sinful (b) establishing a degree of sinfulness— serious or minor, mortal or venial—and (c) explaining the sinfulness as an act in opposition to the natural law or divine law or Church law or a combination of these. Such a systematic approach to morality had the conspicuous merit of setting out with clarity what was acceptable Catholic behavior and what was not. As a child raised in that tradition of morality I had a very clear idea of what was right and what was wrong. It was a world of tidy moral absolutes.

The less attractive side of this approach to morality was a tendency toward a sterile moralism and a trivialization of the sense of sin. If it was a serious sin to break one's fast before receiving Communion and a serious sin to commit adultery, what was it that distinguishes "seriousness"? To make everything a sin was to make nothing a sin. The plain fact of the matter is that a fair amount of traditional moral theology (which was in itself a relatively recent development in the Church) had become a not very convincing morass of casuistry divorced from the roots of genuine spirituality and authentic theology and Scripture study. There has been a shift away from that older theology as a result of that recognition; that "shift away" has been one of the most dramatic revolutions in the history of modern Catholic theology.

The revolution in Catholic moral thinking does not mean that Catholicism has abandoned a moral code. All people live by some code, either articulated by their culture or implicit in their lifestyle, by which they attempt to live both as individuals and as members of the human community. One does not have to be a professing Christian to see that life is not only more tolerable, but better, if people deal honestly with each other, respect the integrity of others, refrain from inflicting pain, and so on. Those rudimentary norms of behavior are found wherever there is civilized human living. However different cultures may be, there is still, at bottom, a fundamental framework within which people live. The absence of such a framework brings not freedom, but chaos and anarchy. The question before us is how, and to what degree, Christianity adds to and/or enriches those basic foundation blocks of individual and social behavior.

That is a very complex issue which a precise example illustrates. We can personalize the issue by simply asking: How do we behave? Our ethical or moral style of life is the end result of a whole series of factors and influences. We learn behavior from our family upbringing, from the expectations of the society in which we live, from the pressures of our peers and our betters, from our cultural, social, and natural environment. What does our religious training add to that? It may simply reinforce what we have learned elsewhere. In school the teachers tried to inspire us to be hard-working, honest, and so on, but many of us had already received that message at home. We were also taught to pray, to avoid "occasions of sin" and to attend Mass. That gave a bit of "Catholic" flavor to our family and school lessons in morality. Catholics had to attend church on Sunday, but we did not think it a sin if the non-Catholic kid next door did not attend church. Did then Catholicism merely add a "Catholic" flavor to general moral norms?

To ask about moral behavior from that angle is to ask about rules and norms of behavior. That may not be the best way of thinking about the Christian life. It may be better to start from an angle which we have insisted on throughout this book: Christian faith is a basic attitude and a basic way of being in the world. From that fundamental starting point—from that worldview, if you will—flows a way of living in the world and a way of doing. Christian faith, to borrow a phrase from theology, involves a fundamental option or choice for God in Christ. To the degree that we choose to act in the world, in conformity with that choice we come closer to acting in the world in conformity with the mind of Christ. We are not trying merely to "do what is right" but to do what is according to the mind of Christ. Through weakness, disposition, distraction, immaturity, or malice we may choose patterns of behavior that are not oriented toward the Gospel. We may recognize those wrong choices, lament them, and try again to hear the Gospel. That, in a nutshell, describes the entire dynamic of continuing conversion. True Christian living, in short, is not to follow a set of rules but to choose to pattern one's life with conscious reference to the person of Christ as we encounter him in faith and through the believing community.

That basic Christian standpoint is easier to articulate in the abstract than it is to implement in the concrete. The full dimensions of what the Gospel demands of us is never fully understood. All of us know that we should not lie or steal or be wantonly cruel to others; we do not need the Gospel to realize that. When the Gospel, however, tells us that we should love our enemies or take up our cross or forgive seventy times seven, we might be taken aback when the demand is recalled just at the time when we do not want to forgive or accept or feel love for someone whom, in fact, we loathe. Christian realism demands that we recognize that we never fully live the Gospel; we only incline toward it through the process of conversion. Here we can take comfort from the history of the Church itself which is, after all, only the history of believers writ large. It took the Church a long time to condemn slavery, to reject racial injustice, and to acknowledge injustices done to women in the Church. The Church as institution had to undergo (and continues to undergo) conversion to a fuller understanding of the Gospel. Our life is burdened by sin and lightened by Christ. We should not be surprised by our failures nor too confident of our successes, but do as St. Paul advises: "Examine yourselves, to see whether you are holding to your faith. Test yourselves" (2 Cor 13:5).

The Church as Moral Teacher

The Catholic Church unapologetically claims the right to "give utterance to, and authoritatively to teach, that truth which is Christ himself, and also to declare and confirm by her authority those principles of the moral order which have their origin in human nature itself."* On the face of it, that does not seem to be an audacious claim. If the Church is the depository of Christian memory and the guardian of the Gospel as well as the vehicle for its transmission, it would seem to follow that the Church should be able to teach its members what is and what is not conformable to Christian living or—for that matter—human living. In fact, throughout its long history, bishops, Popes, theologians, councils, etc., have spoken out on moral matters. In our own country the body of Catholic bishops have spoken on a range of moral matters, from the family and education to racial justice, economics, and matters of war and peace. The American Catholic Church has been at the forefront of the battle against abortions and is closely identified with the "Pro Life" movement. However much others may disagree with those moral utterances, nobody of intelligence has ever denied that it is part of the bishops' functions to engage in such activity.

The fact, then, is that the Church is a moral teacher, and that seems to be a legitimate function of the Church. On that matter there can be no dispute among Catholics. In the formation of the human conscience one must take into account the teaching voice of the Church.

How, in particular, are we to listen to that teaching? Here again we can take into account our own experience. We have no reason to quarrel with the Church for insisting that the ten commandments be observed even if, at times, we do not observe them. Nor should we have problems with the Church proposing a way of acting to which we find a kind of natural resistance. If the Church insists that we love a traditional enemy we may find it difficult to act but we know, viscerally, that it is the voice of the Gospel. But there were times in Church history when the Church proposed a moral norm to which there was widespread resistance because people could not see the evil in an act or because

---

**Declaration on Religious Freedom*, II.14, in *Documents*, p. 695.

such a norm flew in the face of experience. For centuries the Church forbade the taking of interest in lending money. Usury, to use the formal term, was thought to be immoral and contrary to the law of nature. Dante, reflecting the common belief of this time, put the usurers in the same circle of hell as those who committed other kinds of "unnatural" acts. History teaches us that the taking of interest persisted, despite Church prohibitions, through the use of subterfuge and/or casuistry. Finally, in the course of centuries, as economics changed, the ban on usury simply became irrelevant and a dead letter despite the Church's teaching that it was immoral and unnatural.

The parallel case today, of course, is the issue of contraception. We have already mentioned this topic in reference to Church authority. Because it is such a typically "Catholic" issue (no other Christian body forbids it in any and all circumstances) we should look at it again from the perspective of moral living. The traditional ban on contraception was reaffirmed by Pope Paul VI in 1967, and that teaching again has strongly been reaffirmed by Pope John Paul II. What is interesting about this issue is its complexity. It is a moral position which cannot be deduced from either Scripture or the early teaching of the Church. The ban on artificial birth control is deduced from the Catholic reflection on love, marriage, and the finality of sexuality. On the positive side the Church teaches that all sexual acts in marriage must be "open" to the possibility of procreation; otherwise, the act of marriage is somehow defective and imperfect. When married partners have sex, according to this teaching, they must do nothing to impede the *telos* of the act. Without this "openness," the Church argues, there is no way to discriminate married sexuality from, say, homosexual sexuality which is, by nature, not procreative.

The Church's teaching on this matter has met with widespread resistance. It is estimated that in North America over eighty-five percent of Catholics under the age of fifty simply reject the Church's teaching, and an overwhelming number of clergy feel the same. Indeed, as Andrew Greeley has argued, the near total rejection of *Humanae Vitae* has been the watershed event that has compromised the moral authority of the Church in this century.

The question before us, however, is to ask how we can view the Church as a moral teacher when there is such a clear antagonism between what is proposed and what people are prepared to accept. Although we have used the example of contraception, we do not restrict our remarks to that issue. What follow can serve as some safe generalizations.

First, morality cannot be determined by opinion polls. That eighty-five percent of North American Catholics accept contraception as moral does not, of itself, make it moral. When I was a boy growing up in the deep south *everybody* from the pastor of the parish on down thought that racial segregation was morally acceptable. It was not, despite the unanimity. When there is a solid majority for a moral position, especially a comfortable one, then we must listen to hear what the prophetic minority is saying.

Second, what the Church teaches in morality must be heard with utter seriousness. The Church may be teaching from a position which is contrary to the predominant culture, but it must be remembered that the Gospel has strong counter-cultural elements in it. Whether it be an issue like contraception or abortion or economic justice, the basic issue is this: What value is the church trying to transmit in this teaching and how does that value aid us in being conformed more closely to the mind and spirit of Christ?

It is only after the serious person of faith has listened to the Church (and the other sources of moral formation) that a person can form his or her conscience. By conscience we do not mean the "little interior voice" telling us to act or not to act. Conscience is that sense we have of ourselves as moral persons making moral decisions. When we act in conscience we act as authentic human and Christian persons. So—and this is not an evasion since it requires genuine searching—if a person finds his or her authentic conscience at odds with a Church teaching, that person *must* follow his or her conscience rather than the teachings of the Church. We must, as they say, act "in good conscience."

The occasions when our own conscience is in direct conflict with the traditional teachings of the Church are relatively rare. What is far more common is the situation when we agree with the Church in the abstract but find ourselves at odds with that agreement through human factors which seem beyond us. All Christians would agree that monogamous marriage as a permanent state is the ideal proposed by Christ in the Gospels and affirmed consistently by the Church over the centuries. The Christian ideal of marriage is that it should be a covenant of love, a sign of Christ's grace (it is a sacrament), a source of nurture for children, and a mutual pact of love for the spouses. That is the ideal which the Church sets out for all Catholics. Problems arise when—often for reasons which are not only complicated but tragic—a marriage breaks up. Traditionally the Church does not allow a second marriage while one spouse is alive. What has not been well thought out is how to cope with the enormous set of problems arising from such situations where divorces (and remarriages) have taken place. How are we to help the single parent, the children of divorce, and all of the other family problems which arise from the failure of the marriage ideal?

Traditionally the Church's moral positions have been set out after a sustained reflection on the sources of revelation and from the philosophical reflection of the Church on these sources. This has resulted in a morality which is described as divinely authoritative and having the sanction of a rigorously applied metaphysics. The traditional sense of ethics in the Church has been to see moral behavior as guided by a timeless set of principles applicable in all and any circumstances. Now, it is true that we must have some standards against which we measure behavior, but it is likewise true that the very complex fabric of actual life makes it imperative that we continue to seek ways of being faithful to the Gospel and, at the same time, to do justice to the real needs and deficiencies of people. This is not to plead for a "situation ethics" so that morality fits the circumstance. It does mean that the Church should set out an ideal in all of its rigor, without, at the same time, seeming so censorious and insensitive to the real needs of people that they fall away from the community of belief. To balance the values of the Gospel in all of their rigor and the weakness of people and their needs is a delicate task. It is not made easier when from one quarter or another the moral teaching of the Church is used either as a club to stifle dissent or inquiry or as an example of how retrograde the church is. All of us, St. Paul insists, have fallen short of the glory of God; all need God's grace—and none should be denied it.

Social Morality

Catholic theology teaches that every individual, made in the image and likeness of God, is called to be a child of God. Catholic morality would insist that every individual has an obligation to grow in conformity with Christ and that every other person (individual or corporate) has a similar obligation not to impede that growth but to allow it to be nurtured and grown. We are, to use the biblical phrase, our brother's and sister's keeper. That truth can never be fully realized unless we understand that individuals do not live discrete and atomistic lives; all individuals live in societies both intimate (the family, the neighborhood) and large (the state). It follows, then, that the Christian has responsibilities and rights with respect to society while societies have rights and obligations with respect to the individual.

Everything we have said in this chapter earlier about procreative love and the permanence of marriage reflects the abiding concern of the Church for the family. Bernard Cooke has argued, for instance, that in one sense marriage is the basic sacrament precisely because in the union of love between husband and wife we get some sense of God's love for us as humans: a love marked by fidelity and permanence which extends out in time and space. In that sense marriage is not only a liturgical ritual which signifies the sacramental bond but a permanent sign of God's love and fidelity. Cooke writes:

> Building on the transformation of marriage's meaning that began with the Israelitic prophets, Christianity sees the love relationship of a Christian couple as sacramentalizing the relationship between Christ and the church, between God and mankind. This is expressed by and present in the couple's self-giving to each other. They are sacraments to each other, to their children, and to their fellow Christians. This sacramentality, though specifically instanced in Christian marriage, extends to all human friendship.*

This profound sense of the sacredness of marriage and the family leads the Church to insist that the family has certain basic rights which may not be alienated by any power in society, even that of the state. People have a right to marry, to bear children, to provide for their education, to possess the minimum necessary for a human life, to exist without interference of the state. No social power has the right to break up the family, alienate children, or oppress the integrity of the family. On the positive side, it means that the state has the obligation to sustain a society in which it is possible for people to keep the family intact.

Because of the Church's high regard for the family, the basic building block of society, the Church hopes that Catholics will marry within their own tradition. This desire is not a result of Church exclusiveness but a direct consequence of the Catholic sense that the family

---

*Bernard Cooke, *Sacraments and Sacramentality* (Mystic: Twenty-Third Publications, 1983), pp. 93–94.

is the fundamental sustaining unit of both Church and society. The Christian family is central to the self-understanding of the Church. Indeed, the Second Vatican Council call the family the "domestic church."*

It is from the basic regard for the family that all Catholic social ethics flow. Catholic ethics begins with the small unit of the family and looks out to larger realities. All people, both as individuals and as families, have basic rights not only to existence but to human standards of life. The Catholic Church resists the idea that large corporate bodies, private and public, have rights prior to those of the family or the individual. The Catholic suspicion of the totalitarian state rests on its conviction that the individual and the family cannot be made subservient to the state. The dignity of the person cannot be harmed by reasons of either economics or politics. That conviction explains why the Church is often in conflict with the state over the right of the family to educate, to assemble for worship, to keep the family together, and so on.

The defense of individual rights does not mean that the individual is free from corresponding obligations to the state and to society. Catholicism has never preached libertarian anarchy. It recognizes that we are not only born into families but into organized social and political structures. We live, and must live, in the human city. Thus, we have an obligation to be responsible citizens. That does not mean that we can be mindless chauvinists. The phrase "My country, right or wrong" may have a certain vigorous ring to it but it is not a Christian sentiment. We have an obligation to be citizens but we also have the right to resist, by lawful means, the state when it is unjust. The Christian in society must hold the state to the same standard that it maintains for itself: the standard of Christ's teaching.

As a general norm the sense of obligation to the social demands of the state is a simple working out of the Lord's dictum that we should render to Caesar what belongs to Caesar. Where Catholic ethics take on specificity (and complexity!) is the application of general norms to specific circumstances. We see vividly that complexity just by observing the raging debates in the contemporary Church over a wide range of social issues. What is the Christian response to be in the face of naked violence of terrorism by the state or that institutional violence (what the liberation theologians call *violencia blanca*—"white" violence) rooted

---

*The Dogmatic Constitution on the Church, II.11, in Documents, p. 15.

in unjust social institutions? How should Christians react to a government policy of nuclear terror as a threat against enemies? How much can we cooperate with a state which actively fosters immoral practices of one form or another?

Those questions are very complex but one general observation does seem to be in order: While there is ample room for debate about a particular strategy to overcome poverty or aid the elderly or to heighten human rights, there is no question of accepting clearly immoral practices in the name of *Realpolitik*. We can debate strategy but we cannot debate, or be silent in the face of, attempts to suppress human rights or subjugate a people. The Church has the obligation to clearly and firmly state those basic principles that flow from the Gospel. Strategies aside, certain things are not negotiable: you may not torture people in the name of security; you may not starve a civilian population into submission; you may not neglect poor children; you may not allow your elderly to die unattended. It is only after those irreducible principles are articulated that it becomes possible to enter into the debate over strategies.

Because strategies are not always clear it seems at times that Catholic social policy is in disarray. In fact, what often happens in debate is that a closer sense of a coherent policy begins to emerge. For example, it is a basic Catholic principle that innocent human life may never be directly attacked. That principle undergirds the fierce Catholic opposition to abortion. That principle, however, has many specific applications once the principle of respect for life begins to be fully understood. Joseph Cardinal Bernadin has articulated that interrelationship with eloquence:

> It prohibits attacks on the unborn in the womb, direct attacks on civilians in warfare, and the direct killing of patients in nursing homes. Each of these topics in society has a constituency in society concerned with the morality of abortion, war, and the care of the aged and dying. . . . The need to defend the integrity of the moral principle in the full range of its applications is a responsibility of each distinct constituency. If the principle is eroded in the public mind, all lose.*

---

*Cardinal Joseph Bernadin, *The Seamless Garment* (Kansas City: NCR Publishers, 1984), p. 11.

Catholics may debate the strategies for halting war, stopping abortions, or preventing mercy killing of the sick elderly. What is not open for debate is the general ethical principle that innocent life may not be directly attacked. Beyond those bedrock principles Catholic ethics may also extend arguments for a further refinement in ethical thinking that goes beyond basic principles of justice. Historically, the Church has tolerated the execution of criminals as a form of self-protection for society. Since there is a growing consensus today that such executions are not effective and only add to a climate of violence, many Church people agitate for the end of the death penalty. One cannot demonstrate that it is per se immoral to carry out executions under the aegis of a legitimate government. One can argue, however, that the state should relinquish that abstract right in the name of a higher good: the exercise of forgiveness, the expression of hope in the redeemability of all humans, the deepening expression of reverence for all life. Such an argument would appeal to the "Jesus ethic" of charity as something beyond the basic demands of justice. That notion of the order of justice enhanced by the claim of love has been used by recent Popes in their opposition to capital punishment.

The Church and Social Concern

The way we act—the formation of our character and behavior—is most typically shaped by those relationships which are closest to us. We learn to respect, love, and forgive, to deal fairly with and have regard for, from our contacts with our parents, brothers and sisters, relatives, friends, and neighbors. We shape and are shaped by those webs of relationships which encompass family, neighborhood, school, work, and Church. Once, in an argument, someone remarked that what I said was a "typical professor's answer." My antagonist was truly on target; how else could I answer but from the vantage point of what I am—an ordinary professor?

However intimately we are shaped by that which is around us, we must also realize that, as religious people, we are called, and called upon, to be *Catholics,* that is, we are called upon to develop a certain universal sense beyond our immediate social environment. At its very minimum that means that somehow we need to encourage within us a sense of belonging to a reality which is beyond the boundaries of our local existence. To be truly Catholic is to be simultaneously rooted in a local community of believers and consciously part of that larger community with whom we share a common faith. At a practical level of social concern that means that as American Catholics we cannot be blissfully indifferent to those Catholics who live in the impoverished parts of the world, or those who are oppressed by totalitarian governments for their faith, or those who risk their lives for justice in so-called "Catholic" countries below our borders. In a manner which is appropriate to our faith and our circumstances we must accept responsibilities to foster that unity which is exemplified by a common faith. To do less would be an assault on the notion of catholicity itself.

One concrete way in which we can manifest this sense of moral responsibility for the entire Church (and the larger world) is by a commitment to sharing materially and spiritually with those who need us. Catholicism has always had a strong missionary sense; in some ways the history of the Church is the history of missions. Missionary activity means more than preaching to the unevangelized or "saving little pagan babies." To be in mission means to witness the values of the Gospel where those values are absent or undervalued (which could mean everything from a primitive culture to Wall Street), to succor those parts of the world where the needs of the people are great or urgent, and, lastly, to learn from other cultures so that the understanding of the Gospel can be enriched. To be concerned with the universal mission of the Church does not mean simply to send monies to this or that needy group (although we should do that out of a strict sense of Christian love) but to give witness to the values of what we profess as Christians. We may be able, with our wealth, to help with the material needs of the Church in Central America, but a true Catholic should also learn from that area—and others like it—something about our smugness, our wastefulness, our privilege, and our largely unearned abundance. The true Catholic, then, is involved in a give and take situation which involves a going out in mission in order to receive back in faith and understanding.

But, it might be asked, how can this be done by that hypothetical "average" Catholic? There are, of course, many ways of being involved, from making the acquaintance of a missionary group through support to volunteer work in one's own area. One notion that the present author has suggested in a number of his books is for every parish in the developed world to "twin" with a parish in a poor part of the world. This pairing of parishes would then include material support and exchange of information, people, and ideas, as well as other forms of brotherly and sisterly information. Such a procedure would yield both practical results and provide a sense of the unity of the Church.

We cannot rest content with the notion that as North American Catholics our responsibility rests with the giving of our abundance. We must cultivate an impatience with a "two storeyed" Church consisting of a Church which has and one which does not have, a Church which gives and a Church which receives. We must attempt to purify our way of thinking, our language, and our religious priorities in order to see, think, and judge clearly. For all of their alleged failings and excesses, the writers of liberation theology have made one very important contribution to the Church today. They have shown us that our profession of faith and our use of religious language must honestly confront the very harsh and very real situation of the world's poor. These theologians insist that we not use our language of faith as a mask to hide our own complacency. As the Brazilian bishop-poet Pedro Casaldaliga so eloquently phrased it:

> When you say law, I say God.
> When you say peace, justice, love, I say God.
> When you say God, I say liberty, justice, peace.*

Conversion

In the final analysis we can say that the Christian life consists in a series of conversions. All of us, as Christians, are called upon to make a fundamental choice for Christ which means, simultaneously, choosing him and choosing not to turn to those things which impede his presence in our lives. That turning (*metanoia* is the biblical term) is conversion. It is central to the Catholic understanding of conversion that this turning is not a once in a lifetime thing. Conversion, in fact, means a whole life of turning; that series is the very texture of the Christian life. This turning involves:

(a) A turning from sin toward God. At this level conversion is experienced both formally in our liturgical life by going to receive the

---

*Quoted in Leonardo Boff, *Church: Charism and Power* (New York: Crossroad, 1985), p. 24.

sacrament of penance or through our admission of sin in the Sunday liturgy, and informally as we assess the quality of our lives and our need to more fully cooperate with God. The sacrament of penance is a formal and visible way that the Church provides for us to say that we have failed, that we are sorry for those failures, and that we desire to turn once again to God.

(b) Those conversions which help us, under the impulse of God, to advance in the spiritual life. Every step in the life of prayer, in the cultivation of awareness, fidelity, and openness to God, can be seen as a conversion to God in Christ.

(c) Those conversions which occur when we are confronted by choices, often difficult, in life in which it is possible to go beyond the demands of duty in order to more fully express our love for others out of a conscious desire to do the thing which makes us more conformable to Christ.

(d) Cooperation with those special graced times when we may be called to a "second" great conversion in our life which demands a radical reordering of who we are and how we live. It is useful for us to remember that some of our greatest saints underwent such conversions in their lives. St. Teresa of Avila and Mother Teresa of Calcutta had been nuns for years when they underwent a second conversion: Teresa of Avila was led to a greater life of contemplative prayer, while for Teresa of Calcutta it meant total and unrestricted life for the poor. St. Francis of Assisi was leading a life of prayer and penance when he heard the Gospel speaking of living a life of absolute poverty. Such conversions may not be dramatic for everyone but God does call us ever more to conform to his will.

If we think of conversion in terms of a direction in life we can see that conversion means a move *away* from sin and *toward* Christ in such a way that we live closer to Christ *inside* the body of believers with a greater compassion for those who are *outside* the domain of the Church. This multidirectional conversion process can be seen clearly in the life of someone like Thomas Merton, the monk-poet who died in 1968. Disgusted with his early life of aimlessness he turned to Christ in the Church, converted, and became a monk. After some years in the monastery he had a great moment of illumination. He was in downtown Louisville when, in the midst of a crowd of people, he suddenly felt an overwhelming love for people and a sense of solidarity with them. Merton wrote that from that experience he learned that he had to reach out to the needs of the world as a monk and a solitary. That conversion marked a new stage in his spiritual evolution and gave a new direction to his life.*

As we grow in Christ in the Church we slowly begin to understand how we need to be converted to the cries of the world. The Church is not a fortress or a refuge from the world except in the sense that it provides a place to be and a place from which we move out to encounter the world. The authentic Christian does not live in the Church solely for the good of the Church. Although it sounds grandiose to say that we are called to save the world (the Church is so small, the world so large), the plain fact is that Jesus did issue a call for the evangelization of the world. The apostles were called to witness not only on the home turf of Jerusalem but also in ''Judea and Samaria and to the ends of the earth'' (Acts 1:8). That act of witness, fulfilled in different ways, is not separate from the demand that we serve the needs of the world. Jesus insists that in the doing of the works of mercy we preach Christ. Indeed, Christ, in his great eschatological sermon, insists that all of us will be judged, in the last days, according to how we treated the ''least of the brethren'' who, in fact, are signs of Christ in the world (cf. Mt 25:31ff).

It is against the background described above that one must understand the many papal and episcopal messages for international peace, economic justice, and a just social order. Critics argue that such messages are ''political'' and outside the expertise of the Church. Such criticisms miss the point. If the Church is the making real of the presence of Christ in the world, then the Church simply cannot be indifferent (or, much less, hostile) to the genuine needs and aspirations of the world. Catholics, individually or as a class, cannot be walled off from the world in which they live. It is the task of the committed Catholic to understand that there is an intimate connection between what one professes in faith and how one looks out on the world. We must stand ready to have our consciences raised to the sufferings of the world while, at the same time, growing in a conviction that before we give our excess in charity we have a duty *in justice* to allow all of God's children to live in basic human dignity as the person redeemed in Christ.

---

*This process of conversion is amply chronicled in Michael Mott's biography *The Seven Mountains of Thomas Merton* (Boston: Houghton Mifflin, 1984).

Points for Discussion

(a) To what degree have you identified being religious with being moral or, less positively, "obeying rules"? Has this been a mature and helpful way to think of being religious?

(b) What form of behavior most impedes growth in faith as far as you are concerned? Is that a worrisome thing? What strategies have you developed in the face of such behavior?

(c) To what degree has the Church been helpful (harmful) in the formation of a moral outlook on life?

(d) In what sense has the Church been a factor in shaping your social outlook? Can you think of strategies that would give you a keener sense of social justice in the world? How would you relate that to your faith?

(e) Can you state personally a precise meaning for "Christian conversion"? Can you trace out the conversion(s) in your own life? Do you have a sense of Christian growth and maturity? How does that relate to your own sense of moral development in both personal and social morality?

Chapter X

To Be a Catholic

The word *catholic*, derived from the Greek, means "universal." In the first centuries of the Church's history it was used to describe the whole Church as opposed to this or that local manifestation of it. By the end of the third century the word "Catholic" gradually began to mean the universal Church in its teaching and tradition as opposed to a particular heretical sect or a schismatic dissident movement. That is the sense in which St. Augustine of Hippo uses the word. Here is a passage from St. Augustine, speaking about the canon of Scripture, which illustrates his understanding of "Catholic" nicely:

> In the matter of canonical scriptures he should follow the authority of the greater number of catholic churches, among which are those which have deserved to have apostolic seats and to receive epistles. He will observe this rule concerning canonical scriptures, that he will prefer those accepted by all catholic churches to those which some do not accept . . .*

Until the time of the reformation the term "Catholic" meant the orthodox faith of Christianity which, in the famous formulation of Vincent of Lerins, was taught and accepted "everywhere, by all persons, in all places." Catholicity meant, therefore, holding on to the true faith, and it is in that sense that all Christians affirm in the creed a belief in the "one, holy, catholic, and apostolic Church." However, in common parlance today, "Catholic" is usually used to describe that Church which is in communion with Rome, while we use the term "Orthodox" for those Eastern churches which are not in communion with Rome or "reformed" or "Protestant" for those churches which derive in some fashion from the Reformation of the sixteenth century.

Largely as a result of the hostilities of the period of the Reformation the term "catholic" became a theological scene of battle. Roman Catholic theologians in the post-Reformation period began to focus on the meaning of "catholic" as universal and argued that only the

*Saint Augustine, *On Christian Doctrine*, trans. D. W. Robertson, Jr. (Indianapolis: Bobbs-Merrill, 1958), p. 41.

165

Church of Rome possessed that essential mark or character. Their argument was that both the Orthodox and Protestant churches were localized churches restricted in their influence by ethnic considerations or language groups. Only the Roman Church had that universality which Christ wanted for his Church—a universality which was demonstrable in fact (*de facto*) and by right (*de jure*). Such apologists pointed to the widespread existence of Catholicism, its aggressive missionary character, and its uniformity in liturgy and belief.

That apologetical understanding of Catholicity—with very good reason—is not much in vogue today. Its weakness as an argument is patent in that it could be so easily turned back on the Church. If Catholicity is to be described in terms of numbers, geographical distribution, and so on, could that not then be an argument for something like the truth of Marxism which would be able to make similar claims?

Among some Protestant thinkers, the term "Catholic" came to mean, quite simply, the deformation of the Gospel as it became intertwined with the pagan culture of ancient Rome. For such thinkers the Reformation was a purifying event which purged out those pagan and bureaucratic elements which had adhered to the gospel faith of Jesus at an earlier time. For these apologists the events of the sixteenth century, beginning with Martin Luther, literally re-formed the Church into a closer identity with the values of the New Testament.

Most of these older polemics—one still hears echoes of them today—have their roots in the bitter religious controversies of the past—controversies which rent Europe asunder and left a legacy of unseemly religious squabbling. In this more ecumenical period such disputes are on the wane as scholars and other people of good will, both Catholic and Protestant, attempt to better understand the essentials of the Christian faith. We do not wish to enter into those discussions here. For our purposes we will say simply that Catholicism is a mode of being Christian with its own distinctive characteristics. It is that mode and those characteristics which we wish to pursue.

What Does "Catholic" Mean?

In a certain sense we have answered the above question in the earlier chapters of this book. We have emphasized the structural character of the Church, its distinctive Petrine ministry, its emphasis on the sacramental, its conviction that God's presence is mediated to us through sensible realities not excluding the world itself, and its spirit of realism which attempts to steer a path between absolute world denial and basic materialism. Catholics assume, almost unreflectively, that this set of characteristics give tone and substance to the reality of Catholicism. That cluster of characteristics is seen as a "given." But, like all religious sensibilities, that "given" is only retrieved consciously and appropriated existentially by reflection.

For that reason it might be useful to approach our question in a somewhat different fashion. Instead of inquiring into the meaning of being Catholic, we might ask how we might bring our Catholicity to the fore. How, in short, does one become more consciously Catholic?

The answer to that question involves a two-fold reflection that dialectically involves the past and the future. A few words about each.

To be a Catholic is to be a member of a community of memory. This past generation experienced—and continues to experience—a profound revolution in the Catholic Church. It is very difficult to express to a young person today what it felt like to be a Catholic a generation ago. When my students read James Joyce's *The Portrait of the Artist as a Young Man* (a splendid if somewhat crabbed evocation of Irish Catholicism at the turn of the century) it is as if they are reading a description of some arcane kind of Hindu sectarianism. People of a certain age constantly remark, either approvingly or disapprovingly, that the Church is not the same anymore. People have this great sense of disruption and discontinuity.

While great change is a clear and widespread fact in contemporary Catholicism, it is worth noting that, in the midst of change, there is persistent and clear continuity with the Church of the past. It is helpful to recall that Catholics recite the Lord's Prayer before Communion just as the Church did in the second century, they look to the successor of Peter as the guarantor of their oneness in faith as did Irenaeus of Lyons in the second century or Augustine in the fourth. For all of the changes in our parish life, these parishes still preach the Gospel, celebrate the sacraments, bury the dead, minister to the sick, teach the young, counsel the troubled, and succor the poor as they did in the first centuries of the Church.

When, in the search for a greater sense of Christ in our lives, we participate in these "traditional" exercises of the Church we join the great community, studded with saints, heroines, and heroes of the faith, who have done the same thing throughout the past centuries. The exemplary heroes and saints today do to an extraordinary degree what the great exemplars of the faith have always done: Dorothy Day in the 1960s loved the poor with the same intensity as Vincent De Paul did in the seventeenth century; Thomas Merton was a monk and hermit as were the great forebears of the same tradition; Oscar Romero was martyred just like those of the days of ancient Rome; Karl Rahner and Bernard Lonergan are theologians in a tradition of theologians which goes back to the beginnings of the Church. There is, as in most human affairs, more continuity and linkage than discontinuity in the life of the Church.

To live in the tradition of the Church is to witness to the Catholic conviction that Christ's reality can be made present in this world. To live as a Catholic is not only to be a member of the "great" Church today but to have a part of the great Church of the past. It also means that there is a never-ending task of recovering the traditions by which the Church makes Christ present in order to give them actuality and power for today.

To be a Catholic, however, does not mean only to be a link with a past tradition. To be a Catholic is also to be in the present and hopeful toward the future. One thing that both history and common human reflection make clear is that the preaching of God's word and the making present of Christ (the two essential functions of the Church) are not done in a total vacuum. It is a simple but irreducible truth that the Church lives in the texture of history and culture, and it shapes, and is shaped by, that history and that culture. The Catholicism of the Middle Ages is not the Catholicism of the Reformation period which is not the Catholicism of today even when we sense past echoes of those distant eras in our contemporary experience.

That point is important because it leads to a crucial observation: Catholicity means universality but that universality is never a fact; it is always an aspiration. To be a universal Church means that the church in pursuing its essential task cannot tie itself to certain times, certain preferred cultures, certain countries or languages with their own histories and usages. While it is true that the Church has a necessary place and history, it is likewise true that its mission to be universal (catholic) is diminished by any desire to give into the temptation to hold the Church unreasonably to accidents of culture. While we proclaim that our Church is *Roman* it would be a blow to the Church's universality to understand that term in any narrow or constricting cultural terms:

Roman, to be blunt, does not mean exclusively European, Italian, Western and Mediterranean in any Catholic sense of the term.

A concrete example might help to make the point. Africa is one of the great areas of Catholic vitality in the world today. To underscore its importance the Pope (John Paul II) has made a number of pastoral visits to the continent with more planned for the future. The most vexing issue facing the Church in Africa and its leaders is to solve this question: How does one make Catholicism a living reality for Africans without, consciously or unconsciously, insisting upon European cultural patterns which have been a shaping part of Catholicism? This is not an abstract question. The "Africanization" of Catholicism involves questions like these: Should the African clergy remain celibate in a culture where being unmarried is regarded as unnatural and unhealthy? To what elements can indigenous elements like religious dance, respect for ancestors, etc. be incorporated into African liturgical practices? How far can one go in the use of African religious language to recast Christian truths? How does one deal with deep-seated and revered cultural customs like polygamy which seem alien to Christian norms in the West?

It should be obvious that answers to those questions demand a very judicious balancing act in order to insure the integrity of the essentials of Christian revelation and a disentanglement of what is non-essential. It is, of course, easy to say that in the abstract and another thing to put it into practice. It is widely reported, for example, that large numbers of the African clergy (up to and including bishops) are *de facto* married. How respond to that fact? Should one suspend such clerics from their office or ignore the reality or simply change the discipline of the Church? When one looks at the consequences of the choices it is clear that the issue is difficult: to do the first would rob the African church of a large number of its clerics; to do the second (the current policy) smacks of hypocrisy; to do the third would have immense reverberations for the discipline of celibacy in the entire Church.

The specific problems of Africa do not surmount the issue of Catholicity. The Church has always had to balance its need for unity (*not* uniformity) against its requirement of Catholicity.* To grant too much to cultural particularity would be to invite sectarianism in the Church;

---

*The sixteenth century Jesuit mission to China is a vivid example of this problem. The issues that surrounded that mission are brilliantly explored in Jonathan Spence's *The Memory Palace of Matteo Ricci* (New York: Viking, 1984).

to demand too great a uniformity of culture is to diminish Catholicity. To the degree that the Church is faithful to this Catholic mandate it steers a course between those two unattractive alternatives.

Catholicism and Modernity

The problems mentioned above presume that there are people (as in Africa) who are eager to hear the Gospel in the Catholic Church. Catholicism, however, faces differing kinds of problems in different parts of the Church. In the developed Western countries one sees a different set of circumstances. In North America—to focus on the area closest to our own experience—we see a seeming paradox: the explosive growth of fundamentalist brands of Christianity at a time when our social commentators tell us that we are becoming more socially permissive, materialistic, and affluent as a society. Fundamentalism, of course, can be explained as a reaction against this latter development (an attempt to embrace clearly defined standards and beliefs in the face of massive change) but it is not clear that Catholicism has come to grips with this change in society as we experience it today. When we look at our immigrant past in North America it is clear that as a Church we were very successful at adapting to a culture of distress and want. As a Church we nurtured a people with needs and aspirations. The great issue facing the Church today is how we can cope with success and material well-being and not become a class-conscious Church. How, in short, do we become a vital Church of largely middle-class people without alienating Hispanics (who are traditionally Catholic, not fully middle class, and a large American Catholic minority) and others who are not suburban and relatively well-off?

Those are very large challenges. We can take some comfort in the fact that the condition of the Church on this continent is relatively healthy. Nonetheless there are real challenges to our health. Let us mention some of them.

When a priest climbs into a pulpit today he faces a family which, on average, has a television set on seven hours a day in the home. For the Gospel to penetrate (to cut as a two-edged sword as the apostle says) it is necessary to reach us through the welter of words and images which reach us daily, bombarding us with a vision of life that is, by turns, highly attractive and very threatening. One of the greatest problems of contemporary evangelization is to somehow enter a media-saturated atmosphere with something that is "hearable" in a culture which is ever more visually oriented and possessed of ever shorter attention spans.

The omnipresence of the mass media creates other kinds of problems for the Church. There was a time when the family, the Church, the school, and the neighborhood constituted the primary reinforcements of religious, ethical, and social behavior. We well may have disagreed with this or that demand made on us but there were few alternative voices to give us comfort in our dissent. That is hardly true today. Our educators (understood as family, Church, etc.) might tell our young people that casual sex is both socially destructive and morally wrong, but the young person who hears that message need only to turn on the Phil Donahue show to hear an articulate and glib psychologist argue the opposite or slickly produced television clips on MTV vividly illustrating the diametrically opposed point of view.

What a media dominated society has done, in short, is provide a wide range of moral options and choices without any standard to help us make correct choices. The great task of the Church is to somehow enter that world, find a voice in it, be free from its seductions yet open to its rich potentialities, and still speak clearly enough to exercise both a prophetic and an evangelical word to the world. I am not speaking here of television preaching (or, much less, "Christian soap operas" and the like) but of a sharpened sense of the Gospel as it relates to the culture in which we live. The Catholic Church once had to confront the shaping forces of Greek and Roman culture. The great question of antiquity was: "What does Jerusalem have to do with Athens?" The great question today is: "What does Jerusalem have to do with Hollywood?"

The questions and dislocations of modernity are such that large numbers of Catholics, either as a conscious choice or through drifting, simply leave the Church. Everyone knows people who vaguely describe themselves as Catholic but who do so only because their background is Catholic or because that was the religion they were brought up in. We know others who simply leave the Church out of dissatisfaction. Even "regular" Catholics can express vague (or quite specific) dissatisfactions with their faith or feel a certain unease or worry about being Catholic or wonder about the relevance of what to do or who they are. Some ask whether or not it would be possible to be a better Christian without the Church. Still others feel that the Church makes unrealistic demands on them, demands not consonant with their perceptions of life. To put it bluntly: Is being a Catholic worth the effort?

We should say at the outset that such questions are not a sign of spiritual weakness or a symptom of "loss of faith." They are natural byproducts of the times in which we live and part and parcel of the darkness of faith. What, specifically, can we say about these questions and doubts? Those who are convinced of the importance, indeed, the centrality, of Christ in their lives but sense a certain discouragement in the Church need great faith to see beyond the frailties and imperfections of a frail and imperfect Church. It may well be that the greatest test of fidelity to Christ is to see him within the context of the Church itself.

There is yet another point. We have insisted throughout this work that it is *we* who make up the Church; we are the Church. Two facts flow from that simple yet basic assertion. The first is that the Church will never be stronger or holier than the people who make up the Church. Second, and more important, we need to think of the Church as not only providing something for us but, from the other side, as a body which exacts obligations from us. We have obligations toward that community. We simply cannot be indifferent to the "building up of the body of Christ." On this latter point the late Karl Rahner had some very salutary words. He says that only those who are free from self-deceit have the authentic option of choosing against the Church. Rahner writes:

> Quite enough terrible and base things have happened in the history of the church. . . . Where would we go if we left the church? Would we then be more faithful to the liberating spirit of Jesus if, egotistical sinners that we are, we distanced ourselves as the "pure" from this poor church? We can do our part to remove its meanness only if we bear the burden of this wretchedness (for which we all bear some guilt), if we try to live in the church as Christians, if we help to bear the responsibility of constantly changing it from the inside. The church in all denominations must always be the church of the reformation.*

The practical implication of Fr. Rahner's observation is staggering. In essence, what he says is this: we need to see the Church in an authentic manner before we say "no" to it. Are we going to find better resources for prayer outside the Catholic tradition? Are there ways to manifest concretely a love for Christ, and, through Christ, a love for

*Karl Rahner, *The Practice of Faith* (New York: Crossroad, 1983), p. 15.

others outside the Church? Are there authentic alternatives for those who seek a fellowship of community and a sense of Christian tradition? Those questions must be faced by the authentic seeker.

Those questions are not only a challenge for the individual who asks but a forceful examination of conscience for those in the Church who most publicly represent it. How well do they represent the Church? How many people, for example, seek out the practice of TM, join "mystical" sects, or practice Eastern meditation techniques simply because they have never been told about the Church's contemplative tradition? How many others have gone out to "do good" in social action because they cannot seem to connect with the Church's tradition of doing justice and charity? How many people do we know who join fundamentalist churches because they find their own parishes listless in their formality and devoid of any living sense of praise and worship? How many good Catholics have succumbed to the thin gruel of the television preachers simply because they have received not bread but stones from their own pulpits? The list could go on but the point is simple: for reasons ranging from inertia to despair the public Church often hides its light under a bushel of formality and mindless conformity.

The late Peter Maurin, a co-founder of the Catholic Worker Movement, used to say that we have to learn the secret of "exploding the dynamite" of the Gospel. It is a rather vividly violent image but the sentiment that undergirds it is beyond reproof. The Church has an evolved language which it uses in its teaching and in its liturgy; it is a language that derives from, and has its roots in, the Bible. It is a language which is used every day in a welter of languages and accents. But to listen to that language unpacked so that it provokes a response is, for many of us, wish more than reality. For how many generations have we as a people (or how many years have we as individuals) said "forgive us our sins" or "grant us peace" or "teach us to love"? Yet, for many generations and for many years, we have not sought forgiveness or made efforts at peace or tried to love. It is not what the Church preaches that is defective or inhuman but our incapacity and/or unwillingness to transmute words into reality that is at the heart of the problem. Christianity, G. K. Chesterton once said, has not been tried and found wanting; it has simply not been tried. Until we try, we cannot judge it as wanting. The corollary from that is simple. We are never fully Catholic Christians. We are, at best, followers of Christ in the Catholic tradition who try, with the grace of God, to become more universal in our grasp of Christ and more universal in our love of others in Christ. We seek but have not yet fully found; for that reason we are, on this earth, in the role of sojourners and pilgrims.

A Short Credo for Catholics

From its earliest days the Church has summed up its faith in brief credal statements. In the New Testament itself there are brief kerygmas that were formulas of Christian belief, the most ancient being: "Christ died for our sins in accordance with the Scriptures / he was buried / he was raised on the third day according to the Scriptures" (cf. 1 Cor 15:3–4). At every liturgy after the reading of the Scriptures and the homily, we recite in unison a "credo" (from the Latin: "I believe) as an affirmation of our faith in the things we have heard. The great ecumenical councils of the past have formulated creeds as statements and touchstones of orthodox belief. In our own time the late Pope Paul VI formulated and proclaimed a "Credo of the People of God." The great historical creeds are sacred statements, hallowed by time and use.

These historic statements of faith should not deter us from formulating our own private articulations of belief. In one of the last major works, Karl Rahner argued convincingly that the construction of such creeds is not only useful but needed in every age of the faith. Rahner even attempted to set out, briefly, some statements of belief from various perspectives.*

Our intention here is far more modest than Fr. Rahner's. We would simply like to set out some basic statements that are consonant with the issues we have touched on in the pages of this volume. In no way are these to be considered as normative for Catholic faith or even an "ideal" creed. They merely reflect what seems to be central to Catholic faith today. They might serve as a guidepost for fellow searchers and pilgrims. The model I have adopted here is similar to, and influenced by, the manifesto for Christian spirituality written by Kenneth Leech in his magisterial study of contemporary Christian spirituality.**

---

*Karl Rahner, *Foundations of Christian Faith* (New York: Seabury, 1978), pp. 448–59.

**Kenneth Leech, *Experiencing God: Theology as Spirituality* (San Francisco: Harper and Row, 1985), pp. 421–22.

I

We believe that God is and that the vision of God's graciousness must be sustained, lived, and witnessed in our times as it was in the past.

II

We believe in the experience of God in the life and witness of the Jewish people. We affirm that the revelation of God to that people as a God of holiness, justice, and love is the basis for our own ability to believe.

III

We believe that Jesus the Christ is the full and complete revelation of God in history. We affirm that he is God incarnate as well as our fellow pilgrim on this earth.

IV

We believe in, and proclaim fellowship with, the apostolic Church of Peter and the other disciples. We believe that the Church today is sustained and strengthened by the living memory of that apostolic Church in our own midst.

V

We believe that Christ's incarnation is most fully accepted and affirmed when we can "see" that incarnation in the continuing presence of Christ in the ministries of word and sacrament in the Church.

VI

We believe that the Eucharist best exemplifies our unity as children of God in Christ and affirms our desire to make the Eucharist to be the center of our own life.

VII

We believe that Christ is to be seen in our fellows; that when we do it "to the least of the brethren we do it to Christ." We affirm that all men and women are in Christ and that what wounds or demeans them wounds and demeans Christ.

VIII

We believe that we have an obligation, born from faith, to be more fully Catholic, which is to say, more open, more searching, less focused on self, and slow to condemn. We further believe that our failure to be more Catholic requires not only further conversion but open confession of failure both individually and collectively.

IX

We believe, with St. Paul, that God calls all to salvation and, in that light, we believe that the Spirit of God moves in all areas of human life. We believe that to be a Catholic means to be sensitive to the prompting of that Spirit.

X

We believe that we enjoy communion with Mary, the saints, and the faithful of the past as well as those saints who are yet to come. We believe that God is the God of our fathers and mothers as well as the God of the future.

XI

We believe that we are a Church of sinners. We affirm our need for penance and conversion. We further state our hope that we will find, in our death, not alienation from God but eternal life in God.

XII

We believe that on this earth we are the Church. We affirm that our pilgrimage in the Church is a sign, not only of our personal commitment to Jesus the Christ, but of our conviction that we are each called upon to build up the Church which is the body of Christ.

Points for Discussion

(a) Would it be possible for you to set out a personal creed and/or make additions or clarifications to the one which ends this chapter?

(b) What would you describe as the most important facets of being a Catholic as you have experienced them in your own life?

(c) Are you a passive member of the Church? Could you think of ways in which you might enrich the experience of the Church through your life and your activities?

(d) What are some of the ways in which you might cultivate a keener sense of being a member of the universal Church?

(e) Who has been most important in providing you a model for being a Catholic? Can you outline the characteristics, virtues, and attitudes of that person which have been most important to you?

A Select Bibliography

$\mathbf{T}$his short annotated bibliography makes no pretense to completeness. It is merely a first approach for the interested reader so that he or she can pursue subjects in depth.

Abbott, Walter *et al.*, eds. THE DOCUMENTS OF VATICAN TWO (New York: America Press, 1966). A handy edition of the documents of Vatican II in translation.

Adam, Karl. THE SPIRIT OF CATHOLICISM (New York: Doubleday Image, 1954). A classic of pre-Vatican II theology.

Boff, Leonardo. JESUS CHRIST LIBERATOR (New York: Orbis, 1978). Christology from the liberation theology perspective.

Bracken, Joseph. WHAT ARE THEY SAYING ABOUT THE TRINITY? (New York: Paulist, 1979). A useful survey.

Brown, Raymond E. *et al.* PETER IN THE NEW TESTAMENT (New York: Paulist, 1973). An ecumenical study. Basic.

————. MARY IN THE NEW TESTAMENT (New York: Paulist, 1978). An ecumenical study of the scriptural witness to Mary.

Carmody, John/Denise. CONTEMPORARY CATHOLIC THEOLOGY: AN INTRODUCTION (San Francisco: Harper and Row, 1980; rev. ed. 1984). A useful survey from a Rahnerian perspective.

THE CLASSICS OF WESTERN SPIRITUALITY (New York: Paulist, 1978–). A sixty-volume collection of primary sources.

Cooke, Bernard. SACRAMENTS AND SACRAMENTALITY (Mystic: Twenty-Third Publications, 1983). An extremely useful survey of sacramental theology.

Cunningham, Lawrence. THE CATHOLIC HERITAGE (New York: Crossroad, 1983). Catholic history through paradigmatic types.

————. THE CATHOLIC EXPERIENCE (New York: Crossroad, 1985). An extended meditation on being a Catholic.

Curran, Charles. THEMES IN FUNDAMENTAL MORAL THEOLOGY (Notre Dame: Notre Dame University, 1977). Treats the roots of moral theory.

————. TRANSITIONS AND TRADITIONS IN MORAL THEOLOGY (Notre Dame: Notre Dame University, 1979). Some tensions in contemporary moral theology.

de Lubac, Henri. THE SPLENDOR OF THE CHURCH (New York: Sheed and Ward, 1955). A classic study in ecclesiology.

Dulles, Avery. MODELS OF THE CHURCH (New York: Doubleday, 1974). A useful survey of contemporary ecclesiology.

Gilkey, Langdon. CATHOLICISM CONFRONTS MODERNITY (New York: Seabury, 1975). A Protestant perspective on the modern Church and its changes.

Graef, Hilda. MARY: A HISTORY OF DOCTRINE AND DEVOTION (New York: Sheed and Ward, 1963). A useful two-volume historical survey.

Granfield, Patrick. THE PAPACY IN TRANSITION (New York: Doubleday, 1980). Contemporary thinking on the papal office.

Greeley, Andrew *et al.* HOW TO SAVE THE CATHOLIC CHURCH. (New York: Viking, 1984). A program for Church reform.

Grillmeier, Alois. CHRIST IN THE CHRISTIAN TRADITION (New York: Sheed and Ward, 1965). A history of the development of Christology in the early centuries.

Happel, Stephen *et al.* A CATHOLIC VISION (Philadelphia: Fortress, 1984). A brief readable history of the Church.

Hardon, John A. THE CATHOLIC CATECHISM (Garden City: Doubleday, 1975). A useful compendium from a conservative perspective.

Haughton, Rosemary. THE CATHOLIC THING (Springfield, Ill.: Templegate, 1979). A brilliantly readable book.

Hellwig, Monika. UNDERSTANDING CATHOLICISM (New York: Paulist, 1981). A brief and readable introduction.

Irwin, Kevin W. LITURGY, PRAYER, AND SPIRITUALITY (New York: Paulist, 1984). A basic liturgical theology.

Jedin, Herbert, ed. HISTORY OF THE CHURCH (New York: Seabury, 1980). A massive ten-volume survey translated from the German.

Kasper, Walter. JESUS THE CHRIST (New York: Paulist, 1976). A systematic Christology.

Kohmescher, Matthew. CATHOLICISM TODAY (New York: Paulist, 1980). A brief but useful survey.

Küng, Hans. ON BEING A CHRISTIAN (New York: Doubleday, 1976). A comprehensive survey of Christology and the Christian life.

――――. DOES GOD EXIST? (New York: Doubleday, 1978). A voluminous study of the "God problem" in modern culture.

Lonergan, Bernard. METHOD IN THEOLOGY (New York: Herder and Herder, 1972). A classic study in theological methodology. A fundamental work.

Mackey, James. JESUS THE MAN AND THE MYTH (New York: Paulist, 1979). A systematic Christology; readable and contemporary.

McBrien, Richard. CATHOLICISM (Minneapolis: Winston, 1980). An encyclopedic two-volume survey of Catholic belief and practice. Important.

McCormick, Richard. NOTES ON MORAL THEOLOGY 1965 THROUGH 1980 (Washington: University Press of America, 1981). Reprints of surveys of moral problems.

McGinn, Bernard, ed. CHRISTIAN SPIRITUALITY I (New York: Crossroad, 1985). The first of three volumes on the history of Christian spirituality.

Merton, Thomas. NEW SEEDS OF CONTEMPLATION (New York: New Directions, 1961). A classic work by a prolific spiritual master.

Miller, J. Michael. WHAT ARE THEY SAYING ABOUT PAPAL PRIMACY? (New York: Paulist, 1982). A useful survey of the question.

THE NEW CATHOLIC ENCYCLOPEDIA (New York: McGraw-Hill, 1966). Basic fifteen-volume reference tool.

Perkins, Pheme. READING THE NEW TESTAMENT (New York: Paulist, 1978). A basic introduction; useful.

――――. RESURRECTION: NEW TESTAMENT WITNESS AND CONTEMPORARY REFLECTION. (New York: Doubleday, 1984). A fundamental book; scholarly and detailed.

Rahner, Karl *et al.*, eds. SACRAMENTUM MUNDI (New York: Herder and Herder, 1968). A valuable six-volume theological dictionary.

Rahner, Karl. FOUNDATIONS OF CHRISTIAN FAITH (New York: Seabury, 1978). A basic course on Christian theology from a Rahnerian perspective.

――――. THE PRACTICE OF FAITH (New York: Crossroad, 1983). An anthology of Rahner's spiritual writing.

Schillebeeckx, Edward. JESUS: AN EXPERIMENT IN CHRISTOLOGY (New York: Seabury, 1979). A highly technical work.

Schüssler-Fiorenza, Elisabeth. IN MEMORY OF HER (New York: Crossroad, 1983). A fundamental work from a feminist perspective. Important.

Schüssler-Fiorenza, Francis. FOUNDATIONAL THEOLOGY (New York: Crossroad, 1984). A systematic foundational work on Jesus and the Church.

Sobrino, Jan. CHRISTOLOGY AT THE CROSSROADS (New York: Orbis, 1978). A classic of liberation theology.

Sullivan, Francis. MAGISTERIUM (New York: Paulist, 1983). A theological investigation on the teaching authority of the Church.

Tracy, David. BLESSED RAGE FOR ORDER (New York: Seabury, 1975). A study of contemporary theological modes.

————. THE ANALOGICAL IMAGINATION (New York: Crossroad, 1981). A foundational work on theology.

Vorgrimler, Herbert, ed. A COMMENTARY ON THE DOCUMENTS OF VATICAN II (New York: Herder and Herder, 1967/69). For background on the Council, in five volumes.